TALK SMART. HEAL FAST.

Hidden Techniques Revealed

VAIKOM NANDANAN

notionpress.com

INDIA • SINGAPORE • MALAYSIA

ISBN
Paperback 979-8-90342-276-0
Hardcase 979-8-90431-351-7

CONTENTS

ABOUT THE AUTHOR

Vaikom Nandanan is a senior Counselling Psychologist, Clinical Hypnotherapist, and Human Resources Specialist with over five decades of professional experience in India and abroad. His work is rooted in a simple yet profound understanding: prolonged stress affects not only the mind, but also the body—altering inner biochemical balance and gradually disturbing health, clarity, emotional stability, and resilience.

Through counselling, therapeutic meditation, and guided inner techniques, he helps individuals calm the mind, regulate emotional responses, and support the body's natural healing processes. His approach works gently at both levels—psychological and physiological—addressing stress-related concerns such as anxiety, grief, trauma, psychosomatic complaints, immune and autoimmune challenges, chronic emotional fatigue, and work-related burnout.

Alongside clinical practice, he has been deeply involved in leadership coaching and people development within organisations, helping leaders and teams improve emotional awareness, decision-making under pressure, communication effectiveness, and ethical responsibility. His work in corporate and institutional settings bridges psychology and human systems, enabling healthier workplaces and more conscious leadership.

He is also guiding students and young adults in study skills development, concentration enhancement, confidence building, exam anxiety management, and performance-related stress, supporting them not only in academic achievement but also in emotional balance and self-belief during their formative years.

Across diverse settings—clinical, educational, organisational, and community-based—he is conducting emotional intelligence training, stress-relief programmes, and resilience-building interventions for people from all walks of life, consistently emphasising dignity, self-awareness, and inner stability.

During the COVID-19 pandemic, he served as a Voluntary Psychological Support Counsellor under the Government of Kerala's District Mental Health Programme, supporting quarantined individuals and families during a time of intense fear and isolation. For many, his steady voice over a simple phone call brought calm, hope, and the strength to recover when face-to-face support was impossible.

Through his counselling, training, and writing, Vaikom Nandanan reminds us that healing begins when the mind settles, the body regains balance, and a person feels truly heard and understood. He believes that every meaningful conversation—when guided with awareness and care—has the power to restore dignity, resilience, and the will to heal.

AUTHOR'S NOTE

This book emerged not from abstract theory, but from decades of listening to real fear, real grief, and real hope at the edge of human struggle.

Over the years, I have sat across countless individuals—some speaking through tears, some through anger, some through silence. I have listened to parents worried about their children, spouses struggling to understand each other, professionals weighed down by responsibility, and individuals facing illness, loss, or fear that words could barely describe. Again and again, I have noticed something simple yet profound: a single conversation, handled with care, can alter the course of a life.

People often ask me, "What technique do you use?" or "What is your method?"

My honest answer is this: counselling is not a formula. It is presence. It is timing. It is knowing when to speak—and when not to. Over more than five decades as a counselling psychologist, clinical hypnotherapist and human resources specialist, I have learned that healing does not always come from complex interventions. Very often, it begins with listening that feels safe, words that restore dignity, and boundaries that protect trust.

The techniques shared in this book did not emerge overnight. They evolved slowly—through real encounters, moments of crisis, grief, illness, and human vulnerability. Some of these approaches were once shared only in training rooms or supervision discussions. I have chosen to place them here not as secrets or promises, but as **insights shaped by experience and responsibility**.

This book is written not only for professional counsellors, but also for anyone who finds themselves, at some point in life, playing the role of one—a parent, teacher, friend, leader, or caregiver. You may never sit in a counselling room, yet you will almost certainly sit beside someone who needs understanding more than advice.

Talk Smart. Heal Fast – *Hidden Techniques Revealed* is an invitation to communicate with greater awareness, compassion, and ethical clarity. If these pages help you pause before speaking, listen a little deeper, or offer support without harm, then this book has fulfilled its purpose.

Healing does not always require extraordinary knowledge. Often, it begins with **ordinary words used wisely**.

ACKNOWLEDGEMENT

No work of this nature is ever written alone. Though my name appears on the cover, this book carries within it the quiet strength, patience, and encouragement of many who stood beside me—during its creation and throughout the larger journey of life that made this work possible.

My deepest gratitude is to my wife, Lalitha Nandanan, whose unwavering support made this journey possible. Her patience during long hours of writing, her understanding during moments of exhaustion, and her silent confidence in my work sustained me more than words can express. This book would not have taken shape without her steady presence and selfless encouragement.

I am equally grateful to my sons, Jayesh Nandanan and Jitesh Nandanan, and my daughter-in-law, Dr. Onisha Jitesh, who inspired me to transform decades of professional experience into a written form. Their belief that this knowledge should reach beyond consulting rooms and classrooms—to those who genuinely need it—became a powerful motivation for me to begin and complete this work.

My sweet little granddaughters, Shreya and Advika, are my purest inspiration. Their innocence, laughter, and boundless curiosity remind me daily of why healing, understanding, and compassionate communication truly matter. In many quiet moments, it was the thought of the world they will inherit that strengthened my resolve to complete this work.

I offer my profound respect and gratitude to Dr. Bhupendra M. Palan, my Guru and guide in my professional journey. His depth of knowledge, ethical clarity, and disciplined approach to healing shaped not only my professional orientation but also my understanding of responsibility, restraint, and service.

I also bow with reverence to my spiritual guides, Shri Krishnakumar Sthapathy and Dr. Sreelayam Devarajan, whose wisdom, presence, and spiritual grounding enriched my inner journey. Their guidance strengthened my faith in balance, humility, and the deeper dimensions of healing beyond technique.

I offer my heartfelt thanks to my best friend and guide, Shri K. P. Venugopal, whose boundless energy, clarity of purpose, and inspiring commitment to society have been a constant source of strength. His encouragement helped me move forward with steadiness and conviction during times of turbulence, and his faith in purposeful action remains a quiet yet powerful force behind this work.

I wish to acknowledge, with deep gratitude, my friends and beloved fellow members of Senior Chamber International Vaikom Legion, Junior Chamber International Vaikom, Pravasi Sewa, VNICS Dubai, KCTTU, SNDP, and Vaikom Management Association. These associations have been far more than organisations; they have been living communities of friendship, service, and shared values that supported me at crucial moments of life.

There are many charismatic, influential, and compassionate friends and relatives whose faces rise vividly in my memory—Adv. S. D. Suresh Babu, Sidhardhan, Vijayakumaran and Sharad Vijay (USA), Ajith Varma, Sreelatha Ajith, Adv. Muraleedharan, Shiva Prasad, D Narayanan Nair, Er. Rajendran, Rajan Pothi, Manoj YesTech, Manoj Kaimal, Vijayakumar, Soney, Bahuleyan, Anilkumar, Babu M, Viswambharan, PK Venugopal, Ambas & Siddhi, SK Nair, Jagadev Akshara, Nirmal, Jayakumar, Vijayakumar, Shankar, Sreekala and Unnikrishnan, Ajith, Shiburam, Capt. Vinod, Sunil, Sudheer, Saji S. Nair, Unni & Jayathi, Sunil Pillai, Sreekumar, B. E. Mathew & Grace, Adv. Harikumar, Mohandas Damodaran, Sebastian Babu, Biju Kannezhan, Dr. Sasidharan, Jagadeesh Akshara, Pradeepkumar, Dr. Manoj, Adv. Kalesh, Adv. Venu, V. Vijayappan, Geetha Vijayappan, K. P. Byju, Sinu Byju, Binoy P, Rinesh Dasan, Roy & Soly, P. Narayanan, Sindhu Narayanan, M. Reghuvaran, Vijayalakshmi Reghuvaran, Dr. George C, Sabu Varghese, Ambujakshan, Shine, Gopu Iyer, Geetha and Gopakumar, Sharad Soman, Mrs. Amruthakumari, Vidyadharan, Anirudhan, Er. Saifuddin, Raju, and many others.

They stood behind me like strong supporting pillars, offering encouragement, belief, and timely strength. During periods of fierce personal and professional avalanches, their presence ensured that I did not fall—but instead found the courage to stand tall and move forward.

This book is offered with humility and gratitude, shaped not only by professional practice but also by love, friendship, guidance, spiritual grounding, and collective goodwill. To all who have walked beside me—named and unnamed—I offer my sincere thanks.

May this work serve as an instrument of healing, understanding, and balance—and may it be guided always by grace, wisdom, and compassion.

ETHICAL AND PROFESSIONAL DISCLAIMERS

The case examples, names, situations, and identifying details presented in this book are not real and do not refer to any specific individual. They are either composites drawn from multiple professional experiences or have been substantially altered to protect confidentiality.

Any resemblance to actual persons, living or deceased, or to real events or places, is purely coincidental. The purpose of these illustrations is educational—to convey psychological principles and therapeutic approaches—not to document real-life cases.

This book is not intended as a substitute for medical, psychiatric, or emergency care. The techniques and insights shared here are meant to complement—not replace—professional diagnosis, medication, or treatment by qualified healthcare providers.

Readers experiencing severe psychological distress, psychiatric illness, or medical emergencies are strongly advised to seek appropriate professional help.

The counselling approaches described in this book are presented within the ethical scope of professional counselling and psychological support. Readers are reminded that the application of any technique must be guided by their own professional training, licensure regulations, and local laws.

Not all techniques are suitable for all clients, contexts, or conditions. Professional judgement, supervision, and referral remain essential.

Individual responses to counselling and therapeutic techniques vary widely. The outcomes described in case illustrations should not be interpreted as guaranteed results.

Healing is influenced by many factors, including individual readiness, physical health, emotional context, and ongoing support systems. No method works uniformly for all individuals.

The techniques described in this book are not intended for unsupervised self-application by readers, especially in cases involving trauma, grief, psychiatric illness, or altered states of consciousness.

Practising counsellors and therapists should apply these approaches only within the limits of their training and ethical competence. Lay readers are encouraged to seek professional guidance rather than attempt therapeutic interventions on themselves or others.

References to spiritual, cultural, or philosophical traditions—including Indian wisdom—are offered as interpretive frameworks, not doctrinal truths. Readers are free to engage with these perspectives in ways that align with their own beliefs and values. No spiritual belief system is promoted as superior or universally applicable.

Laws and professional regulations governing counselling, psychology, and mental health practice vary across countries and jurisdictions. Readers are responsible for ensuring that their professional practice complies with the laws and ethical guidelines applicable in their region.

The author and publisher assume no liability for misuse or misapplication of the material presented.

INTRODUCTION

There are moments in life when a single conversation can change the course of a person's journey. I have witnessed this countless times in my work as a counselling psychologist, clinical (medical) hypnotherapist, and human resources management specialist, over a career spanning more than five decades in India and abroad.

People have walked into my counselling room carrying years of pain, confusion, or silence. Often, what they needed was not medicine, not advice, and not complicated theories—but a safe space where they felt heard, accepted, and understood.

Let me begin with a story.

A young man once came to me restless and hopeless. On the outside, he appeared successful—good grades, a promising future. Inside, however, he was falling apart. His parents urged him to "be strong" and "focus on success," but he felt empty and lost, unable to explain what was wrong. He had withdrawn from friends, avoided family conversations, and had even considered ending his life.

During our first session, he barely spoke. His silence filled the room, and his eyes carried a weight heavier than words. Many would have rushed to ask questions or offer solutions. Instead, I chose to simply sit with him. After a few moments, I said softly,

"It's okay. You don't need to explain everything right now. Just know you are safe here."

That was the turning point.

Tears rolled down his face, and for the first time, he allowed himself to release emotions he had locked away for years. Slowly—through patience, guided imagery, and counselling techniques—he began to rebuild his sense of self. Weeks later, he told me,

"It wasn't your words that healed me. It was the way you listened and made me feel understood."

That experience reaffirmed what I have always believed: counselling is not about giving advice—it is about creating a healing space where transformation happens naturally.

Another story remains close to my heart.

A middle-aged woman once sought my help. To the world, she appeared cheerful and accomplished. Behind her smile, however, lived years of quiet suffering. For decades, she had devoted herself entirely to her family—her husband, her children, her home. In the process, she had slowly lost touch with her own dreams and identity.

"I don't know who I am anymore," she confessed one day. "I feel invisible."

Her pain was not dramatic. It was subtle, hidden beneath routines and responsibilities. She was not clinically ill, yet she was emotionally exhausted. Through gentle conversations, therapeutic meditation, and reframing exercises, she began reconnecting with herself. She rediscovered her long-forgotten love for painting and timidly began again.

One day, she brought me a small canvas filled with bright flowers.

"This may look simple," she said, "but for me, it is proof that I am alive again."

That painting was not just art—it was the return of her spirit.

This story reminds us that counselling is not only for those in visible crisis. It is also for those who appear "fine" on the outside but are silently yearning for meaning, balance, and self-discovery.

These and many other experiences have shaped the heart of this book.

Talk Smart. Heal Fast – Hidden Techniques Revealed is written in simple, accessible language, combining scientific understanding with the warmth of lived practice. It presents counselling as both a science and an art—the science offering structured methods and evidence-based tools, and the art guiding how they are applied with compassion, sensitivity, and creativity. No two people are the same, and no healing conversation should be either.

This book is written for:

- counsellors, psychologists, psychiatrists, and doctors seeking to deepen their practice
- students of psychology who wish to see theory come alive in real-life contexts
- teachers, parents, leaders, and helpers who guide others through struggle
- administrators, managers, supervisors, and public officials who work with people, conflict, and responsibility
- anyone who wants to understand others better and offer meaningful support
- and most importantly, anyone seeking clarity, healing, or personal growth

In the chapters that follow, you will discover:

- how the human mind and emotions shape daily life
- the essentials of effective counselling communication—listening, questioning, silence, and presence
- practical tools such as reframing, guided imagery, and relaxation techniques
- advanced approaches including therapeutic meditation, trance work, and emotional release
- real-life case insights showing how healing unfolds in practice
- evolved techniques developed and refined over decades of experience

If you are a professional, may this book offer fresh perspectives and usable insights.

If you are a student, may it help you blend compassion with skill.

If you are a parent, teacher, or leader, may it guide you to touch lives with greater empathy.

And if you are silently struggling, may these pages remind you that you are not alone—and that healing is always possible.

As we begin this journey together, I invite you to read not only with your mind, but also with your heart. Counselling is not merely about solving problems. It is about awakening possibilities—helping people rediscover their strength, their meaning, and their joy.

Let us now step into the world of psychological counselling—where science meets empathy, where technique meets compassion, and where every conversation holds the power to heal.

CHAPTER 1

UNDERSTANDING PSYCHOLOGICAL COUNSELLING – FOUNDATIONS AND THE HUMAN MIND

The Role of Counselling in Modern Life

Life often brings us to crossroads where the mind feels heavier than the body. We may appear successful outwardly—career progressing, family responsibilities fulfilled, social image intact—yet inwardly struggle with sleepless nights, unspoken stress, or the quiet ache of feeling misunderstood.

In such moments, what we often receive are familiar, well-intentioned phrases: *"Be strong." "Don't worry so much." "This too shall pass."*

But while advice may comfort for a moment, it rarely penetrates the deeper layers of pain, confusion, or doubt. This is where psychological counselling begins—not as advice, but as a process of guided discovery, healing, and growth. As Carl Rogers wisely said, *"The good life is a process, not a state of being. It is a direction, not a destination."* Counselling is about helping individuals find that direction, guiding them to understand their thoughts, emotions, and behaviours, and empowering them to make choices aligned with their well-being.

Psychological counselling is as ancient as human thought, yet it remains vital today. Every culture has nurtured methods to guide the mind—be it through the wisdom of the Upanishads in India, Socratic dialogues in Greece, or meditation practices in China. Modern counselling bridges classical wisdom and contemporary science, helping people navigate challenges of daily life, trauma, and stress.

With more than fifty years of professional experience in Psychological Counselling, Clinical Hypnosis, and Human Resources Management,

I have witnessed the transformative power of counselling across diverse contexts. From corporate boardrooms to personal crises, the principles remain consistent: attentive listening, empathetic presence, and structured guidance.

Counselling, Advice, and Therapy – Understanding the Differences

While counselling often overlaps with advice and therapy in everyday understanding, the distinctions are important. Advice is directive: it tells someone what to do, often based on the adviser's perspective. Therapy, in the medical sense, particularly in psychiatry, involves clinical diagnosis and treatment, often including prescription medication, with the primary aim of correcting mental disorders.

Counselling, however, is a scientific and empathetic exploration of the mind. A Counselling Psychologist functions as a scientist of thought and emotion, observing patterns, uncovering underlying beliefs, and guiding the client toward insight and self-directed change—without using medication. Psychotherapy, which falls under the domain of trained psychologists, employs structured methods such as Cognitive Behavioural Therapy (CBT), Rational Emotive Behaviour Therapy (REBT), Person-Centred Therapy (PCT), and Solution-Focused Brief Therapy (SFBT). These approaches are applied with clear objectives: to modify thoughts, behaviours, and emotional responses, enabling the client to achieve practical and lasting change.

By understanding these distinctions, individuals—whether clients or professionals—can approach the right form of support confidently. Counselling is not a sign of weakness; rather, it is a powerful tool to navigate life's challenges, enhance self-awareness, and foster resilience in both personal and professional domains.

Overcoming Stigma and Misconceptions

One of the most persistent barriers to seeking counselling is stigma. Many clients fear that others will label them as "mentally ill" or "weak" if they reach out for psychological support. They may hide their sessions even after experiencing positive results, silently carrying their progress without sharing it.

Through my years of counselling, I have observed that addressing these fears directly is crucial. Creating an environment of trust, confidentiality, and normalization helps clients feel safe. Framing counselling as personal growth, professional development, and resilience training can make it socially acceptable and appealing, especially for corporate leaders, officials, and managers who may initially hesitate to seek support.

For instance, a mid-level manager struggling with workplace stress may fear judgment from colleagues. By reframing the session as a "leadership resilience coaching" experience, the same techniques of guided reflection, emotional awareness, and stress management can be applied without invoking stigma. Over time, clients realize that seeking guidance is a strength, not a weakness, and that everyone, regardless of status, benefits from structured support for the mind.

Exploring the Mind – Conscious, Subconscious, and Beyond

Understanding the mind is foundational for effective counselling. Indian psychology identifies multiple layers: conscious, subconscious, para-conscious, universal conscious, and supreme conscious. *(Please see next chapter for mor details).*

In counselling, awareness of these levels enables interventions that respect the client's mental and spiritual layers. Techniques such as guided imagery, reflective questioning, and mindfulness facilitate access to deeper layers, supporting change at both thought and experiential levels.

Counselling Across Time and the Chemistry of Experience

When we speak of counselling as an ancient art, we are not being poetic—we are tracing a human practice that has always adapted to new crises. The dialogues of the Upanishads taught seekers through question and silence. Socrates, in Athens, taught through questions that led listeners to examine their lives. In the modern era, Freud and Jung drew maps of the unconscious; Carl Rogers reminded us that presence and acceptance often heal in ways no instruction can.

Telephonic Counselling During Covid – Voices from the Other End

During this period, I provided day-and-night telephonic counselling to thousands of patients. Some were struggling with the fear of losing loved ones; others battled sleeplessness, isolation, or relentless panic attacks. Through these conversations, I once again witnessed the immense power of the human mind to restore balance when guided with clarity and steadiness.

One of the most effective approaches I used was deceptively simple: inviting clients to revisit intensely positive, meaningful moments from their lives—moments when they had felt deeply safe, loved, valued, and alive.

A woman who had lost her father to Covid was drowning in grief. Her voice trembled as she spoke; her breathing was shallow and uneven. On the phone, I gently guided her step by step to revisit her wedding day—the moment when her father had blessed her with tears of pride and joy. I asked her to describe the scene in detail: her bridal attire, the fragrance of flowers, the music in the background, the warmth of her father's trembling hands.

As she immersed herself in that memory, something shifted. Her breath slowed. Her tone steadied. Grief did not disappear—but it softened, held now within a wider emotional field of love and gratitude.

Another young man, struggling with panic after testing positive, was hyperventilating as he spoke to me. His thoughts were racing toward worst-case scenarios. Instead of arguing with his fear, I guided him to recall the birth of his first child. Within minutes, as he visualised holding his baby and breathing in that first scent of newborn skin, his breath steadied. Later, he told me that the "fear of death" had gradually melted into a renewed "desire to live," as his body felt flooded again with life-affirming biochemical messengers.

These experiences reinforced something I had long observed in clinical practice: emotions are not abstract states. They are biological events.

The Collective Biochemical Messenger System

Over decades of counselling, I began to understand emotional healing not only as a psychological shift, but as a coordinated biological rebalancing. What we call emotion is carried throughout the body by what I describe as the Collective Biochemical Messenger System—an integrated network of signalling pathways linking mind and physiology.

This system includes:

- Neurotransmitters such as dopamine, serotonin, and GABA, which regulate mood, reward, and calm.
- Neuropeptides, including endorphins, influencing pain, pleasure, and resilience.
- Hormones such as oxytocin and cortisol, shaping bonding, stress response, and alertness.
- Immune mediators, including cytokines, which connect emotional states with inflammatory and healing processes.

Together, they form a psycho-neuroendocrine–immune symphony—a living chemical signature of our inner experience.

Every emotion generates a distinct biochemical pattern. Joy, safety, and love activate one constellation of messengers. Fear, panic, and despair activate another. Importantly, the brain does not sharply distinguish between a present event and a vividly re-experienced memory. When a meaningful memory is recalled with sensory richness, the associated biochemical pattern is reactivated, influencing breathing, heart rate, muscle tone, immune signalling, and mood.

In this sense, counselling is far more than conversation. It is guided modulation of the Collective Biochemical Messenger System.

Practical Application for Readers

When used responsibly, this understanding transforms the counselling process.

By guiding attention, memory, reflection, and imagery, the counsellor becomes a steady conductor—helping shift the client's internal biochemical landscape from distress toward regulation.

Steps for Practice:

1. Invite the client to recall a deeply positive, meaningful memory.
2. Encourage sensory immersion—sight, sound, touch, scent, and emotional tone.

3. Ask them to observe changes in their body—breathing, voice, posture, muscle relaxation.
4. Anchor the state with a simple gesture (placing a hand on the chest, gently clasping fingers).

With repetition, the mind–body system learns to access stabilising biochemical patterns more readily. This builds resilience without dependency. It strengthens emotional regulation while supporting immune balance and physiological recovery.

What appears to be "just a conversation" may, in reality, be a subtle reorchestration of the body's internal chemistry.

And when guided with care, this inner orchestration becomes one of the most powerful pathways to healing.

Key Takeaways and Practical Exercises

Key Takeaways

1. Counselling is a universal tool:
2. Seeking guidance is a mark of strength, not weakness. It helps navigate personal stress, career pressures, and interpersonal challenges, making it relevant for leaders, managers, and officials.
3. Distinguish counselling from advice and therapy:
4. Counselling explores thoughts, emotions, and behaviours to foster insight and change.
5. Advice gives directive solutions based on the adviser's perspective.
6. Therapy involves clinical diagnosis and treatment, often including medication.
7. Stigma exists but can be mitigated:
8. Many avoid counselling fearing judgment. Normalizing it as personal growth or professional development increases acceptance and willingness to engage.
9. The mind has multiple layers:
10. Conscious: Current awareness and decisions.

11. Subconscious: Hidden beliefs and habits.
12. Para-conscious: Intuition and emerging insights.
13. Universal conscious: Shared archetypes and collective unconscious (Jung).
14. Supreme conscious: Higher awareness and universal wisdom.
15. Understanding these layers enables effective guidance and deeper insight.
16. Emotions have a biochemical signature:
17. Neurotransmitters, hormones, neuropeptides, and immune molecules form patterns corresponding to emotional states. Vividly recalling positive experiences can reproduce beneficial patterns, reduce stress, and enhance resilience.
18. Guided memory recall is a practical tool:
19. Structured exercises focusing on joyful, meaningful memories can induce positive emotional and physiological changes quickly and effectively.

Practical Exercises for Leaders and Officials

These exercises are designed for real-life use—whether you are a corporate leader, school principal, government officer, administrator, or community organiser.

1. Daily Decision Review (5 Minutes at Day's End)

At the end of your day, sit quietly and write down:

- Three important decisions you made today.
- Ask yourself:
    - Did I decide calmly?
    - Was I reacting to stress or pressure?
    - Did habit influence me more than clarity?

Over time, you will begin to notice patterns—where stress overrides wisdom, or where patience improves outcomes. Awareness itself begins to change behaviour.

2. Positive Memory Reset (Emotional Rebalancing Exercise)

When you feel overwhelmed:

- Close your eyes for 5–10 minutes.
- Recall a moment when you handled a challenge successfully.
- It may be:
    - A difficult project completed well
    - A crisis your team overcame
    - A moment of appreciation from someone you helped

Bring in sensory details:

- What did you see?
- What did you hear?
- How did your body feel at that moment?

Notice your breathing. Notice your posture.

This helps your body re-access constructive biochemical patterns associated with confidence and calm.

3. Listening Without Fixing (Empathy Practice)

In your next one-on-one conversation:

- Allow the other person to finish speaking fully.
- Do not interrupt with advice immediately.
- Reflect back what you heard:
    - "It sounds like you felt overlooked."
    - "You seem frustrated with how this unfolded."

Notice how simply feeling understood reduces defensiveness.

Presence often solves what authority cannot.

4. The Two-Breath Reset (In-the-Moment Stress Control)

Whenever tension rises—in meetings, during conflict, before a major decision:

- Take two slow, deep breaths.
- Feel the air entering and leaving your body.
- Notice where tension sits—jaw, shoulders, chest.

Do not change anything. Just observe.

This brief pause allows the rational brain to re-engage before you speak.

5. Emotional Trigger Mapping (One-Week Awareness Exercise)

For one week, keep a small notebook or digital note.

Each time you feel irritated, anxious, or defensive:

- What happened?
- Who was involved?
- What did you feel physically?
- How did you respond?

At the end of the week, look for patterns.
Do certain personalities trigger you?
Does criticism affect you strongly?
Does lack of control disturb you?

This awareness prevents repetition of automatic reactions.

6. Shared Success Recall (Team Resilience Builder)

During a team meeting, remind your group of a past success:

"Remember how we handled that major deadline together?"
"Recall how we stayed calm during that unexpected crisis."

Invite them to briefly describe what worked well.

This activates collective confidence.
Teams function better when they remember their own strength.

You may even create a small, shared gesture—a clap, a hand-on-heart, or a simple phrase—to anchor that memory.

These practices are not theoretical tools.
They are daily disciplines that gradually transform leadership from reactive to reflective, from pressured to purposeful.

Footnote:
The *Collective Biochemical Messenger System (CBMS)* is an integrative clinical framework proposed in this book to describe the dynamic interaction between psychological experience and physiological regulation through interconnected neurobiological pathways. It refers to the coordinated activity of neurotransmitters (e.g., dopamine, serotonin, GABA), neuropeptides (e.g., endorphins), hormonal systems (e.g., cortisol, oxytocin), and immune mediators (e.g., cytokines), which together translate emotional states into measurable biological responses.

Contemporary research in affective neuroscience and psychoneuroimmunology supports the bidirectional relationship between mental states and bodily processes. Emotional experiences are mediated by limbic–cortical networks and expressed through neurochemical signalling (LeDoux, 1996; Panksepp, 1998). Stress responses involve activation of the hypothalamic–pituitary–adrenal (HPA) axis and sympathetic nervous system, influencing endocrine and immune functioning (McEwen, 2007). Furthermore, evidence indicates that immune signalling molecules such as cytokines interact with neural circuits affecting mood and behaviour (Dantzer et al., 2008). Research on neuropeptides highlights their role in linking emotional experience with bodily states (Pert, 1997).

Within this framework, emotionally charged memories—particularly when vividly recalled—can reactivate associated neural and biochemical patterns, thereby influencing autonomic regulation and subjective mood states. While the term *Collective Biochemical Messenger System* is not a standard diagnostic or laboratory construct, it is used here as a clinically integrative concept to describe the functional unity of these systems in therapeutic contexts.

CHAPTER 2

SELF-AWARENESS, UNDERSTANDING HUMAN BEHAVIOUR, AND PRACTICAL COUNSELLING TECHNIQUES

Life often presents challenges that reveal not only what we do, but who we truly are. Early in my career, a corporate executive, Ramesh, came to me distressed. His team was underperforming, deadlines were slipping, and he found himself snapping at colleagues. Despite outward success, he couldn't understand why he reacted so strongly.

This is where self-awareness becomes critical. Ramesh's conscious mind saw the problems—missed deadlines, underperforming employees—but it was the deeper layers of his subconscious and para-conscious mind that triggered automatic reactions. In counselling, we often observe that the mind carries old patterns of fear, insecurity, or unresolved conflict. Without awareness, these patterns operate invisibly, yet they influence behaviour, relationships, and decisions profoundly.

Through guided reflection, Ramesh began to recount specific situations in which he reacted with anger—moments in meetings, conversations with juniors, even casual remarks that unexpectedly triggered irritation. Rather than analysing or correcting him immediately, I invited him simply to observe these incidents as if watching a recording of his own behaviour.

Gradually, without judgement or self-criticism, he began to notice a familiar pattern beneath the surface reactions: a subtle but persistent fear of failure rooted in his early career experiences, when mistakes had been met with harsh scrutiny. Each time someone questioned him, his body responded as though he were once again standing before a critical superior. His mind interpreted the present through the lens of the past, and his emotional–biochemical system reacted accordingly—tightened muscles, quickened breath, a surge of defensive energy.

What he had interpreted as "others being careless" was often his own anxiety resurfacing in disguise.

As this awareness deepened, something significant shifted. The next time irritation rose within him, he recognised it sooner—almost at its birth. That recognition interrupted the old biochemical cascade before it gathered full force. In that brief pause, his breathing steadied, his posture softened, and clarity returned.

And in that space, he discovered choice. He could respond thoughtfully rather than react impulsively. What once felt automatic and involuntary gradually became conscious, regulated, and manageable.

Understanding human behaviour is not just academic—it is practical. Humans make decisions through rational thought, emotional responses, and habitual conditioning. Counselling explores these layers to help clients understand why they think and act as they do.

During the Covid pandemic, I counselled thousands of individuals via telephonic sessions. Anxiety, fear of death, and grief were pervasive. One young nurse was overwhelmed by guilt for surviving when colleagues had fallen ill. Though her conscious mind knew she wasn't responsible, subconscious guilt haunted her. Guided reflection on positive memories—moments of helping patients, smiles, and gratitude—gradually shifted her emotional state.

This illustrates the power of collective biochemical patterns—specific combinations of neurotransmitters, hormones, neuropeptides, and immune molecules corresponding to emotional states. Vivid recall of positive experiences recreates beneficial biochemical patterns, producing relief, calm, and resilience.

In corporate settings, a project manager, Anita, repeatedly experienced frustration when team members missed deadlines. Reflecting through counselling, she realized she was projecting her own fear of failure onto her team. Awareness of this pattern allowed her to experiment with supportive communication rather than criticism, resulting in improved team collaboration and reduced stress.

The Five Levels of Mind in Indian Psychology

Understanding the mind's different layers helps us make sense of thoughts, feelings, and behaviours. In Indian psychology, the mind operates at five levels:

1. Conscious Mind – What we are aware of in the moment: thoughts, sensations, and perceptions. When reading this book, you are consciously processing words and meaning. In counselling, we often start by exploring what clients can articulate at this level.
2. Subconscious Mind – Stores memories, habits, and patterns that influence behaviour without our awareness. Ramesh's quick anger in the boardroom, for example, was driven by subconscious patterns from early experiences. Counselling techniques like reflection, journaling, or CBT help access and reshape these patterns.
3. Para-conscious Mind – Between conscious and subconscious, containing emerging thoughts, intuitions, and "gut feelings." For instance, a leader sensing tension in a team without explicit signs may be noticing para-conscious cues. Observing these hints can guide better decisions.
4. Universal Consciousness – Connects individual awareness with broader collective experience. Carl Jung's collective unconscious in modern psychology aligns with this level. Archetypes, instincts, and shared human patterns influence reactions even unconsciously. During Covid counselling, many patients shared similar fears, reflecting universal emotional patterns.
5. Supreme Consciousness – The highest level, associated with spiritual insight, intuition, and a profound sense of purpose. Counselling can guide individuals to align with this level, gaining perspective and resilience in challenging times.

Practical Application:

- Leaders: Recognize that team members may react based on subconscious patterns. Observing recurring behaviour and gently exploring underlying causes guides positive change.
- Individuals: Self-reflection can bring subconscious and para-conscious patterns into awareness, allowing conscious choices instead of automatic reactions.
- Counsellors: Tailor interventions: CBT targets conscious/subconscious thoughts, PCT explores para-conscious levels, and solution-focused approaches can connect with universal or higher conscious perspectives.

Example: A client feared all family members would fall ill during Covid. By exploring subconscious/para-conscious triggers—past illness experiences—and guiding focus toward universal resilience patterns, the client gradually reduced anxiety. Visualizing positive outcomes and recalling coping successes also engaged higher conscious processing, creating calm and clarity.

Counselling Techniques in Everyday Life

1. Cognitive Behavioural Therapy (CBT)

CBT teaches that thoughts influence feelings and behaviours. Negative thinking is identified, challenged, and replaced with realistic alternatives.

Example: Raj believed, "I will fail at my new job." By listing past achievements, he reframed it as: "I have the skills to learn and grow." Confidence improved, anxiety reduced.

2. Rational Emotive Behaviour Therapy (REBT)

REBT addresses irrational beliefs like "Everyone must like me." These beliefs are logically challenged and replaced with rational thinking.

Example: Meera, a team leader, thought disagreement equals failure. She replaced it with: "Disagreements are opportunities to learn," reducing anxiety.

3. Person-Centered Therapy (PCT)

PCT emphasizes that people can find solutions if truly heard. Counsellors provide empathy and acceptance, facilitating self-discovery.

Example: A student stressed about exams found clarity through supportive, non-judgmental listening, creating a practical study plan.

4. Solution-Focused Brief Therapy (SFBT)

SFBT emphasizes solutions and small actionable steps. Past successes are leveraged to reach desired outcomes.

Example: During Covid, a father stressed about home routines imagined a collaborative family plan. By replicating small past successes, household harmony improved.

Key Takeaways

1. Self-awareness is foundational.
2. Behaviour reflects beliefs; patterns often reside subconsciously.
3. Assessment tools reveal tendencies, not labels.
4. CBT and REBT help reframe negative thinking.
5. PCT shows empathy and listening can unlock solutions.
6. SFBT focuses on solutions, not problems.
7. Collective biochemical patterns influence emotional states.
8. Incremental change is more sustainable than abrupt transformation.

CHAPTER 3

EMOTIONS, EMOTIONAL INTELLIGENCE, AND BEHAVIOURAL PATTERNS

Life is an orchestra of experiences. Each day brings its own instruments—work, relationships, memories, expectations. Yet the true conductor of this orchestra is often unseen: our emotions. They set the tempo of our thoughts, the intensity of our reactions, and the rhythm of our behaviour.

Early in my clinical practice, a mid-level corporate manager named Arjun contacted me in visible distress. He had recently been promoted—a moment that should have brought pride and excitement. Instead, it brought persistent anxiety, irritability, and exhaustion. Sleep eluded him. Minor mistakes by colleagues provoked sharp reactions. Quietly, almost shamefully, he began questioning his own competence.

Outwardly, Arjun appeared successful. Inwardly, he was struggling to stay afloat.

Arjun's experience is far from uncommon. Many people assume emotions are fleeting moods that come and go. In reality, emotions—when unrecognised or unmanaged—quietly shape our decisions, influence our relationships, and even leave their imprint on the body. They determine how we interpret events, how we respond to stress, and how we relate to ourselves.

Understanding how emotions arise, how they interact with thoughts, and how they translate into behaviour is not merely an academic exercise. It is the foundation of practical counselling, emotional intelligence, and genuine self-mastery.

1. How the Brain Processes Emotions

Modern neuroscience offers valuable insight into why emotions feel so immediate and, at times, overwhelming. The brain processes emotional experiences through two primary pathways—each serving a distinct survival function.

a) The Short (Fast) Pathway

At the heart of this pathway lies the amygdala, a small but powerful structure within the limbic system. The amygdala functions as an early-warning system, scanning the environment for potential threats.

When we perceive danger—such as a heated argument with a colleague or a sudden critical remark—the sensory input first reaches the thalamus. From there, a rapid signal is sent directly to the amygdala. This route bypasses detailed reasoning. The response is immediate and automatic.

Within milliseconds, the body reacts. Heart rate increases. Muscles tense. Adrenaline and stress hormones surge through the bloodstream. Emotion arrives before thought, preparing the body to fight, flee, or freeze.

Example:

During the Covid period, many clients reported sudden waves of panic upon hearing that a family member had tested positive. Even before medical details were known, the amygdala triggered fear responses—tight chest, racing thoughts, shallow breathing. Rational assessment had not yet begun, but the body had already entered survival mode.

This pathway is fast because it is ancient. It evolved to protect life. But in modern contexts, it often reacts to perceived threats rather than real ones.

b) The Long (Deliberate) Pathway

Running alongside this rapid system is a slower, more reflective pathway involving the prefrontal cortex—the part of the brain responsible for reasoning, judgment, and conscious decision-making.

In this pathway, sensory information travels from the thalamus to the cortex, where it is analysed in depth. Memory, context, past experience, and probability are all considered. This allows the brain to ask: *Is this truly dangerous? What is the appropriate response?*

Crucially, the prefrontal cortex can regulate or even override the amygdala's automatic alarm. When engaged effectively, it transforms impulsive reactions into thoughtful responses.

Example:

Arjun initially reacted with instant anger when a team member made a mistake. His amygdala interpreted the error as a threat—to his reputation, his authority, his new role. Through awareness practices, he learned to pause before reacting. In that pause, he began asking different questions: *Is this mistake critical? Is it intentional? How would guidance work better than blame?*

Over time, this deliberate engagement of the long pathway allowed him to respond with calm direction instead of frustration. The same situation, processed differently, produced a completely different outcome—for him and for his team.

Key Insight

Emotional intelligence begins with recognising this dual processing system.

When we become aware of the short pathway's immediate reactions and consciously activate the long pathway's reflective capacity, we shift from being driven by emotion to *working with* emotion. Behaviour then becomes a choice rather than a reflex.

This awareness does not suppress emotion. Instead, it honours its signal while allowing wisdom to guide action. In counselling and in life, this is where true self-regulation begins.

2. The Limbic System and Amygdala in Everyday Life

The limbic system, with the amygdala at its centre, governs much of our emotional life. It stores emotional memories, scans for danger, and prepares the body for survival. Because it operates largely outside conscious awareness, many people believe their strong emotional reactions are "out of their control."

In counselling, one of the first liberating realisations for clients is this: *what feels uncontrollable is often simply unrecognised.* When emotional reactions are understood as limbic responses rather than personal failures, shame reduces and choice becomes possible.

Example from ordinary life:

During a family dinner, Priya felt a sudden surge of irritation when her sibling teased her lightly. On the surface, the remark was playful. Her conscious mind knew this. Yet her body reacted instantly - tight jaw, flushed face, sharp words forming on her tongue.

As we explored the moment, Priya recalled a childhood incident when the same sibling had publicly mocked her during a vulnerable moment. That memory, stored quietly in the limbic system, had been reactivated. The amygdala was responding not to the present tease, but to an old emotional wound.

Once Priya recognised this, something shifted. The irritation no longer felt mysterious or overpowering. She learned to pause, take a breath, and remind herself: *This is now, not then.* Over time, she could respond with calm humour instead of snapping. Awareness transformed reaction into response.

Example from a corporate context:

Sunil Kumar, a senior CEO, noticed a similar pattern in himself. During board meetings, even mild criticism triggered disproportionate anger. His voice tightened, his responses became defensive, and the atmosphere in the room shifted.

By understanding the role of the amygdala, Sunil realised that negative feedback activated an old fear of failure rooted in early professional experiences. Before responding, he began practising a brief grounding technique—slow breathing combined with conscious posture relaxation. This simple pause allowed the prefrontal cortex to engage. As a result, he could listen more fully, respond thoughtfully, and prevent conflicts that might otherwise have escalated.

These examples reveal a crucial truth: the limbic system reacts quickly, but it can be regulated. Awareness does not erase emotion—it places it in context.

3. Emotional Triggers and Behavioural Patterns

Emotions rarely arise in isolation. They are often triggered by earlier experiences, deeply held beliefs, or subconscious patterns formed over time. These triggers act like hidden switches—activated by present events yet powered by the past.

For counsellors and individuals alike, recognising emotional triggers is essential. Without this awareness, people repeatedly react without understanding why. With it, patterns begin to loosen.

During the Covid period, many clients reported intense fear whenever they heard news of rising infection numbers. One woman, Sunita, described feeling paralysed each time she checked the news. Her heart raced, her chest tightened, and catastrophic thoughts took over.

As we explored this fear, Sunita made an important connection. Her reaction was not solely about Covid statistics. Years earlier, she had watched her father suffer through a prolonged illness. Hospitals, medical updates, and waiting periods had become emotionally charged symbols of helplessness and loss.

Her present fear was echoing that unresolved memory. Once she recognised this link, the panic began to soften. She could say to herself: *This fear belongs partly to the past. I am responding to memory as much as to reality.* With this reframing, her anxiety reduced, and she regained a sense of inner steadiness.

Behavioural Patterns

When emotional triggers are activated repeatedly, they solidify into behavioural patterns. Over time, these patterns shape personality, influence decisions, and colour relationships.

For example:

- Persistent irritability may lead a person to withdraw from teamwork, gradually isolating themselves.

- Excessive worry can result in procrastination, as the fear of failure paralyses action.
- Unchecked fear may produce chronic indecisiveness, where even small choices feel overwhelming.

These patterns are not character flaws. They are learned emotional responses that once served a purpose. Counselling helps individuals recognise these patterns, understand their origins, and gently reshape them.

When emotions are understood rather than fought, behaviour begins to change naturally. This is where emotional intelligence moves from theory into lived experience.

4. Emotional Intelligence: Concept and Application

Emotional intelligence is not a personality trait one is born with; it is a skill that can be developed through awareness and practice. At its core, emotional intelligence refers to the capacity to recognise, understand, manage, and influence emotions—both our own and those of others.

In everyday life, emotional intelligence determines far more than intellectual ability. It shapes how we handle pressure, how we relate to people, how we recover from setbacks, and how we lead ourselves and others through uncertainty. In counselling, it becomes one of the most practical tools for healing and growth.

Emotional intelligence is commonly understood through five interrelated components. These are not isolated abilities; they work together, much like instruments in an orchestra.

- **Self-awareness** is the foundation. It is the ability to notice emotions as they arise—before they spill into words or actions. A person who is self-aware can say, *"I am feeling anxious,"* or *"I notice irritation building inside me,"* without immediately acting on it.
- **Self-regulation** follows awareness. Once an emotion is recognised, self-regulation allows a person to pause, steady themselves, and choose an appropriate response rather than reacting impulsively. This does not mean suppressing emotion; it means guiding it constructively.

- **Motivation** refers to the capacity to use emotions in the service of meaningful goals. Instead of being derailed by fear or frustration, emotionally intelligent individuals learn to channel emotional energy toward perseverance, purpose, and resilience.
- **Empathy** is the ability to sense and understand the emotional states of others. It goes beyond sympathy. Empathy allows one to listen without judgement, to recognise unspoken feelings, and to respond with sensitivity rather than assumption.
- **Social skills** are the outward expression of emotional intelligence. They involve communicating clearly, managing conflict, building trust, and sustaining healthy relationships—whether in families, workplaces, or therapeutic settings.

Example from Practice

During the pandemic, I worked with a nurse who was experiencing intense emotional strain. She was caring for critically ill patients while suppressing her own fear. Initially, her anxiety expressed itself through irritability and emotional exhaustion.

Through counselling, she began by recognising her internal state—naming the anxiety rather than dismissing it (self-awareness). She learned simple breathing and grounding techniques that allowed her nervous system to settle during moments of overwhelm (self-regulation). Rather than withdrawing, she reminded herself why she had chosen her profession and refocused on the meaning of her work (motivation).

As her own fear softened, she became more attuned to the emotional distress of her colleagues (empathy). She adjusted her communication—speaking more gently, listening more patiently, and offering support rather than criticism (social skills).

The result was not only personal relief but a visible shift in team morale. Her emotional intelligence did not eliminate stress, but it transformed how she and those around her navigated it.

Emotional intelligence bridges inner awareness and outer behaviour. In counselling, it becomes the language through which emotions are understood rather than feared. As individuals strengthen these five capacities, they gain not only emotional balance but the ability to respond to life with clarity, compassion, and choice.

5. Practical Exercises to Enhance Emotional Intelligence

Emotional intelligence does not grow through insight alone. It develops through small, consistent practices that train awareness, regulate reactions, and gently reshape habitual responses. The following exercises are simple, yet powerful, because they work with the mind and body together.

Mindful Pause

When an emotional trigger arises, the first step is not action, but recognition. Pause for a moment and silently name what is happening: *"This is anger,"* or *"This is fear."*

By labelling the emotion, you shift it from an unconscious force to a conscious experience. This simple act reduces its grip and creates space between feeling and behaviour. Over time, the pause becomes a natural interruption to impulsive reactions.

Emotional Journaling

At the end of the day, briefly record emotionally charged situations. Note what happened, what you felt, how you reacted, and how you might respond differently next time. When reviewed weekly, these entries reveal recurring triggers and patterns that often go unnoticed in daily life.

Journaling is not about judging yourself; it is about observing yourself with curiosity. Patterns, once seen clearly, begin to loosen on their own.

Perspective Shift

When conflict arises, make a deliberate effort to imagine the other person's internal state. Ask yourself: *What might they be afraid of? What pressure might they be under?*

This exercise does not excuse harmful behaviour, but it cultivates empathy. When perspective widens, emotional reactivity softens, and communication becomes more constructive.

Biochemical Regulation through Positive Recall

The body does not distinguish sharply between real experiences and vividly recalled ones. By consciously recalling moments of joy, safety, or success—such as a meaningful achievement, a loving interaction, or a peaceful scene—you activate beneficial neurochemical patterns associated with calm and resilience.

This practice helps counterbalance stress-driven biochemical responses and trains the nervous system to access steadiness even under pressure.

Together, these exercises strengthen emotional intelligence not by force, but by repetition and awareness. They teach the mind and body a new rhythm—one that favours clarity over reactivity.

6. Integrating Levels of Mind with Emotional Management

To understand emotional reactions fully, it is helpful to view the mind as operating at multiple levels. These include the conscious, subconscious, para-conscious, universal, and supreme levels of mind. Emotions rarely originate only at the conscious level. More often, they arise from deeper layers shaped by memory, instinct, and accumulated experience.

- The conscious mind is where thoughts are recognised and decisions are made.
- The subconscious mind stores emotional memories, beliefs, and learned responses.
- The para-conscious bridges instinct and intuition, often influencing reactions before they are clearly articulated.
- The universal and supreme levels offer perspective beyond the personal—connecting individual experience to shared human patterns and deeper awareness.

Emotional reactions often begin in the subconscious or para-conscious layers, triggered by memories or associations long before conscious reasoning engages. Counselling helps bring these hidden influences into awareness, allowing choice to replace automatic response.

Example – Corporate Context:

Rahul, a project lead, frequently felt sudden frustration when a team member missed deadlines. Consciously, he wanted to remain patient and supportive. Yet irritation surged almost instantly, tightening his voice and posture.

Through guided reflection, Rahul recognised that this reaction was linked to earlier experiences with a previous manager who had been harsh and unforgiving. His subconscious had learned to associate missed deadlines with criticism and threat. Once aware of this pattern, Rahul began noticing the earliest signs of irritation—tight shoulders, shallow breath. He paused, grounded himself, and reframed his response, saying: *"Let's review this together and find a solution."*

Over time, his reactions softened. His team noticed a calmer, more collaborative leadership style, which improved both morale and productivity. Awareness at deeper levels of mind had reshaped outward behaviour.

Example – Ordinary Life:

During the Covid period, a mother named Anjali experienced repeated anxiety when her child resisted online learning. Consciously, she knew she should remain calm. Yet worry surged quickly, often turning into impatience.

As we explored this, Anjali realised her anxiety was linked to her own childhood schooling experiences, where academic pressure had been intense. These subconscious memories were being reactivated. Through mindfulness and visualisation exercises, she recalled times when she had successfully overcome challenges despite fear. By accessing these positive internal patterns, she could regulate her emotional responses more effectively.

Gradually, her home environment became more supportive and less tense. The shift did not come from suppressing emotion, but from understanding its deeper origins and guiding it consciously.

When emotional management integrates all levels of mind, reactions lose their urgency and meaning replaces impulse. Counselling, at its best, helps individuals move fluidly between awareness, reflection, and response—allowing emotions to inform life without dominating it.

Connecting to Higher Consciousness

Beyond conscious thought and emotional regulation lies a deeper dimension of awareness—often referred to as *supreme consciousness.* Across spiritual traditions and philosophical systems, this dimension is described not merely as a mental state, but as an expanded field of awareness that connects the individual to something greater than the personal self. It does not negate emotion, nor does it suppress human experience. Rather, it offers a wider horizon from which experience can be understood. When individuals touch this broader awareness, personal fear begins to loosen its grip, and life is no longer perceived as an isolated struggle but as part of a shared and meaningful human journey.

During telephonic counselling with a Covid-affected patient, this shift became evident. He was overwhelmed by fear—not only of illness, but of uncertainty, loss, and helplessness. Rather than focusing on symptoms alone, I gently guided him to reflect on shared human experiences: survival through past crises, the resilience visible across generations, and the remarkable adaptability that has enabled humanity to endure adversity repeatedly. As his attention moved from "Why is this happening to me?" to "This is something human beings have faced and overcome before," his panic began to soften.

This insight did not arise from reassurance alone. It unfolded as his awareness expanded beyond the immediacy of personal fear into a deeper recognition of continuity—of life, resilience, and meaning that extends beyond individual circumstances. The calming that followed was not merely psychological; it was experiential. His breath slowed, his thoughts cleared, and a steadier presence replaced panic.

Supreme consciousness, in this sense, is not simply a cognitive reframing mechanism. For many, it represents a profound dimension of being—whether understood spiritually, philosophically, or existentially—that anchors the individual in something larger than momentary distress. It does not deny suffering, nor does it magically remove difficulty. Rather, it offers perspective rooted in connection, trust, and continuity. From that vantage point, fear loosens—not because danger disappears, but because awareness expands.

7. Applied Emotional Intelligence in Professional and Personal Contexts

Emotional intelligence becomes truly transformative when applied in real-life situations. Whether in leadership roles or everyday relationships, the ability to recognise, regulate, and respond wisely to emotion shapes outcomes far more than technical skill alone.

Corporate Leaders and Officials

Scenario 1 – High-Stakes Board Meeting

The boardroom was quiet in that particular way only high-stakes meetings become quiet—polite, tense, charged beneath the surface. Slides had just been presented. Targets had been reviewed. Then came the comment.

"Neha, this strategy seems short-sighted. Have we miscalculated?"

The words were measured, but the implication stung.

In an instant, her body reacted before her mind could organise itself. Her jaw tightened. A pulse throbbed at her temple. Heat rose to her face. The short emotional pathway had activated—swift, protective, defensive. Years ago, she might have responded sharply, correcting the speaker, asserting authority, silencing dissent.

But this time, she noticed.

She felt the surge without obeying it.

She placed both feet firmly on the floor beneath the table. One slow breath. Then another. As her exhalation lengthened, the grip in her chest loosened. The deliberative pathway of the brain began to engage.

She silently reframed the moment:
This is information, not attack.
This is about the strategy, not about me.

When she spoke, her voice was steady.

"That's an important concern. Can you help me understand which aspect appears most vulnerable?"

The room shifted. Shoulders lowered. The conversation deepened instead of hardening. By the end of the meeting, what could have become a fracture became refinement.

Later, a board member told her quietly,
"Your calm response changed the entire direction of the discussion."

Emotional intelligence, in that moment, was not theory. It was leadership under pressure.

Scenario 2 – Team Conflict Resolution

The tension in the department had become almost tangible. Emails were curt. Meetings ended abruptly. Productivity was slipping.

Vinod could have issued warnings. He could have reassigned tasks. Instead, he chose to observe before acting.

He noticed that one employee, Arjun, became defensive whenever deadlines were questioned. The other, Kavita, grew visibly anxious when ideas were challenged. Beneath their sharp exchanges lay something softer—and more fragile.

In individual conversations, he listened without interruption.

Arjun finally admitted, "I'm scared of looking incompetent. I worked hard to get here."

Kavita whispered, "When my suggestions are dismissed, I feel invisible."

The conflict was not about deadlines or reports. It was about fear—fear of failure, fear of insignificance.

When Vinod brought them together, he did not begin with accusations. He began with awareness.

"It seems both of you care deeply about doing well," he said gently. "But fear may be speaking louder than collaboration."

As they recognised their subconscious triggers, something shifted. Blame gave way to understanding. Defensive tones softened.

Emotional intelligence, in this setting, was not authority imposed from above. It was insight applied with care. And insight restored balance without escalation.

Ordinary Individuals

Scenario 1 – Family Dynamics

Sita carried an invisible weight every day.

If the kitchen was not spotless, she felt inadequate.
If homework was incomplete, she felt negligent.
If she rested for even a short while, guilt whispered, You are not doing enough.

No one else accused her. The pressure came from within—a subconscious belief that love must be earned through perfection.

During our work together, she began with something simple yet powerful: naming her emotions.

"This is guilt."
"This is fear of being judged."
"This is the old voice telling me I must prove myself."

As she observed without condemnation, she noticed how these emotions tightened her chest and quickened her movements. Her emotional–biochemical system was constantly in a subtle state of stress, even when nothing urgent was happening.

Through guided reflection, she uncovered early experiences where praise came only after flawless performance. Her nervous system had learnt that imperfection meant rejection.

We then practised visualising ordinary, imperfect family evenings—shared laughter over simple meals, unfinished chores waiting patiently, children smiling without evaluation.

Gradually, her body responded differently. Her breath softened. Her shoulders lowered. She experimented with small shifts—delegating tasks, accepting "good enough," allowing herself to sit without explanation.

What changed was not merely her schedule.

Her inner dialogue transformed from accusation to kindness.

"I am doing enough."
"My worth is not measured by spotless counters."

Emotional intelligence, in her case, did not create a perfect household. It created a more peaceful mind. And from that peace, healthier relationships naturally followed.

Scenario 2 – Health Anxiety During the Pandemic

The fear did not come quietly. It circled his mind day and night.

"What if my wife gets infected because of me?"
"What if my children lose their father?"
"What if I stop breathing while they are asleep?"

Though his symptoms were mild, his imagination was severe. Every cough became a warning. Every news report became confirmation. He was not only fighting a virus—he was fighting catastrophic images that replayed endlessly in his mind.

When he spoke to me over the phone, his voice trembled with urgency. He was not asking about oxygen levels or medication. He was asking for certainty—something no one could honestly give.

Instead of challenging his fear, I redirected his focus gently.

"Tell me," I asked, "have you ever faced a crisis before—something that felt overwhelming at the time?"

There was a pause. Then he spoke of an earlier chapter in his life—losing his job unexpectedly years ago. He had feared financial ruin then. Yet he had rebuilt, learned new skills, and eventually created greater stability than before.

As he narrated that story, something subtle shifted in his tone. His breathing slowed. His sentences became clearer. The same mind that had been generating worst-case scenarios was now recalling evidence of strength.

We deepened that memory.

"What helped you survive that period?"
"Who stood by you?"
"What did you discover about yourself?"

Each answer activated not fear—but resilience.

Physiologically, the change was visible even over the phone. The sharp, shallow breathing softened into steadier rhythm. The tremor in his voice reduced. His emotional–biochemical system, which had been flooded with stress signals, began shifting toward patterns associated with calm, confidence, and relational connection.

As his nervous system settled, rational thinking returned. He stopped compulsively checking alarming news. He began focusing on practical steps—hydration, rest, isolation protocols, reassuring his children with steady language instead of visible panic.

Fear had not disappeared. But it was no longer driving him.

Emotional intelligence, in that moment, became a bridge—from anxiety to agency.

Across professional and personal settings, emotional intelligence performs this quiet but profound transformation. It does not eliminate pressure, uncertainty, or loss. It changes how the individual stands in their presence.

Instead of reacting automatically, one pauses.
Instead of being ruled by fear, one observes it.
Instead of collapsing into emotion, one regulates it.

In that shift—from reaction to response—lies the difference between turbulence and steadiness, between escalation and clarity.

Emotional intelligence is not merely a skill set.
It is the disciplined art of guiding emotion—rather than being governed by it.

8. Practical Techniques to Enhance Emotional Mastery

Emotional mastery does not emerge from suppressing feelings or forcing control. Suppressed emotion does not disappear—it merely waits. True mastery arises from awareness, understanding, and skilful response.

Over the years, I have observed that transformation rarely depends on complicated methods. Rather, it grows from a handful of simple practices applied with consistency. When individuals learn to recognise emotional activation early, understand the thoughts that sustain it, and gently guide their inner biochemical responses, profound shifts begin to occur.

Mindful Observation

Every emotion first speaks through the body.

Before anger becomes words, the jaw tightens.
Before anxiety becomes panic, the breath shortens.
Before disappointment becomes withdrawal, the shoulders slump.

These signals are not enemies; they are early messengers. When individuals learn to notice these bodily cues without judgement—almost as a curious observer—they interrupt the automatic emotional cascade at its earliest stage.

In that moment of noticing, something powerful happens. The short, reactive pathway slows. The longer, reflective pathway awakens. The body begins to settle before the mind escalates.

Emotional mastery begins not with control, but with noticing.

Cognitive Reframing (CBT / REBT)

Once awareness is present, the next layer reveals itself: thought.

Many emotional storms are intensified not by events themselves, but by the meanings we attach to them:
"This will go wrong."
"I am failing."
"They are against me."

These thoughts often arise so quickly that they feel like facts. Yet when gently examined, they are interpretations—not truths.

Cognitive reframing does not demand artificial optimism. It invites balanced realism. The question shifts from "What if this is a disaster?" to "What evidence do I have?" or "Is there another possible explanation?"

When interpretation changes, emotional chemistry changes.
When emotional chemistry shifts, behaviour follows.

Thought is not merely mental—it is biochemical instruction.

Emotion Labelling

There is quiet power in naming what we feel.

"This is anger."
"This is fear."
"This is disappointment."

When emotion remains vague, it dominates. When it is named, it becomes defined—and what is defined can be regulated.

Labelling creates gentle psychological distance. The person is no longer engulfed by emotion; they are observing it. Neuroscience suggests that naming feelings activates regulatory regions of the brain, softening limbic reactivity. In lived experience, it feels like stepping back just enough to breathe.

Clarity reduces intensity.

Solution-Focused Action (SFBT)

Emotion becomes overwhelming when it feels endless.

One of the most stabilising interventions is identifying a single, immediate action—small, practical, doable.

Make one phone call.
Take one deep breath.
Clarify one sentence.
Correct one minor error.

Action restores agency. Even modest movement signals to the nervous system: I am not helpless. I can respond.

Emotional mastery strengthens not through endless analysis, but through meaningful forward motion.

Visualization and Positive Memory Recall

The mind–body system does not fully distinguish between present experience and vividly recalled memory.

When individuals recall a moment of genuine confidence, love, safety, or accomplishment—engaging sight, sound, sensation—the body begins to reproduce the same emotional–biochemical pattern associated with that original event.

Breathing slows.
Posture straightens.
Voice steadies.

This is not imagination as fantasy. It is memory as regulation.

By intentionally activating beneficial emotional patterns, individuals train their internal system toward resilience rather than reactivity.

Empathic Dialogue

Emotional mastery does not end within the self; it extends into relationship.

In moments of tension, responding with immediate correction often intensifies conflict. But reflecting emotion first—"It sounds like this has been frustrating for you," or "I can see you're overwhelmed"—changes the dynamic.

When people feel understood, their nervous system settles. Defensiveness lowers. Dialogue becomes possible.

Empathy regulates both the speaker and the listener. It transforms confrontation into connection.

Example – Pandemic Scenario

During a session with a front-line healthcare worker, exhaustion and fear were colliding within her. She spoke of chaotic wards, constant alarms, and the dread of making one irreversible mistake.

Rather than analysing stress levels, I invited her to recall a specific moment when her team had successfully managed an overwhelming patient load.

At first, she hesitated. Then she began describing the coordination, the silent understanding among colleagues, the relief when a patient stabilised.

As she spoke, her breathing slowed. Her shoulders softened. The strain in her voice eased.

What changed was not the hospital environment—but her internal state. The memory activated biochemical patterns associated with competence, trust, and resilience.

In subsequent shifts, she reported clearer thinking and steadier decision-making—even under pressure.

Emotional mastery, in that moment, was not about eliminating stress.
It was about shifting from reactivity to grounded strength.

When practised consistently, these techniques transform emotional turbulence into emotional resilience—allowing individuals to guide their inner responses rather than being governed by them.

9. Emotional Intelligence Tools and Assessments

While self-awareness often begins through reflection, structured tools can deepen insight. Used wisely, assessments do not define a person—they illuminate patterns.

Self-Report Inventories

Instruments such as the Trait Emotional Intelligence Questionnaire or the Schutte Self-Report Emotional Intelligence Test (SSEIT) offer individuals a structured way to reflect on emotional awareness, regulation, empathy, and interpersonal effectiveness.

These tools are not diagnostic labels. They are mirrors—snapshots of current tendencies. When approached with curiosity rather than defensiveness, they reveal strengths to build upon and blind spots to gently address.

Practical Application

Assessment becomes meaningful only when translated into daily life.

A leader who recognises impulsivity may practise deliberate pauses before meetings.
A professional who scores lower in empathy may consciously reflect emotions before offering solutions.
An individual noticing stress sensitivity may integrate brief breathing rituals into daily routines.

Insight becomes growth when it shapes behaviour.

Observational Assessment

Emotional intelligence is also cultivated by observing others carefully and compassionately.

Patterns of withdrawal, irritability, over-control, or avoidance are rarely random. They often signal underlying fear, insecurity, or unmet need.

When observation replaces assumption, communication softens.

Example

In one organisation, a team member repeatedly avoided open disagreement. In meetings, she nodded quietly, rarely challenged ideas, and often withdrew when discussions became tense. Over time, unresolved issues accumulated. Frustration grew among colleagues. Some labelled her disengaged. Others described her as indifferent.

But behaviour is rarely what it first appears to be.

When explored gently, a different story emerged. Earlier in her career, expressing disagreement had led to public criticism. Her nervous system had learned a protective lesson: silence is safer than confrontation. What looked like passivity was, in fact, anxiety. Avoidance had become her shield.

The manager, once aware of this, changed his approach. Instead of demanding opinions in front of the group, he began inviting her perspective privately first. In meetings, he normalised disagreement by saying, "Different views help us think better." He acknowledged contributions openly and respectfully.

These small shifts signalled psychological safety.

Gradually, she began to speak—not dramatically, but steadily. Her insights proved thoughtful and precise. As her confidence strengthened, the team dynamic shifted. Conversations became more balanced. Resentment dissolved. Productivity improved.

The transformation did not come through authority or correction.
It came through understanding the emotional roots beneath behaviour.
Emotional intelligence, in this instance, was not a technique.
It was perception refined by empathy.

Closing Integration

Together, structured assessments and mindful observation offer a balanced and mature pathway toward emotional intelligence. Formal tools provide measurable insight—highlighting tendencies, strengths, and blind spots. Lived observation adds nuance—capturing tone, hesitation, posture, silence, and context.

One without the other is incomplete.

Measurement without humanity becomes rigid.
Observation without reflection becomes vague.

When integrated, they honour both science and experience—both the measurable dimensions of emotion and its lived, embodied reality.

Emotional mastery, then, is neither mystical nor mechanical. It is not achieved through rigid control, nor through vague inspiration. It is cultivated through disciplined awareness—returning, again and again, to observation, reflection, and gentle recalibration.

At first, this awareness feels deliberate.
Later, it becomes familiar.
Eventually, it becomes natural.
And when steadiness becomes natural, emotion is no longer something that overwhelms.
It becomes something that informs, guides, and strengthens.

That is the quiet power of emotional intelligence in practice

10. Common Emotional Challenges and Counselling Interventions

In counselling practice, emotional challenges rarely appear in isolation. Anxiety often hides beneath anger, guilt may disguise itself as over-responsibility, and grief may silently shape behaviour long after loss is acknowledged. Recognising these emotional patterns—and responding to them with appropriate, humane interventions—is central to effective counselling.

Anxiety and Panic

Anxiety is one of the most frequent concerns brought into the counselling space. Clients describe racing thoughts, tight chests, trembling hands, and an unshakable sense of impending danger. Panic, in its acute form, overwhelms the nervous system and convinces the person that control has been lost.

In such moments, the primary goal is not analysis but regulation. Breathing techniques with prolonged exhalation help calm the autonomic nervous system. Relaxation exercises signal safety to the body. Positive memory recall—inviting the client to relive moments of calm, competence, or joy—stimulates beneficial biochemical responses that counteract stress hormones. Once the body settles, the mind becomes receptive to reflection and reassurance.

Anger and Frustration

Anger often masks deeper emotions such as fear, helplessness, or unmet needs. Left unchecked, it damages relationships and reinforces negative self-concepts. Counselling interventions begin with identifying triggers—specific situations, words, or memories that ignite anger disproportionately.

Clients are guided to pause at the earliest bodily signals of anger: clenched jaws, tightening shoulders, rapid speech. Visualization techniques help them imagine possible outcomes of reacting impulsively versus responding consciously. This shift—from reaction to response—restores choice and dignity, allowing anger to become information rather than destruction.

Guilt and Regret

Guilt can be constructive when it guides ethical behaviour, but when excessive or misplaced, it becomes corrosive. Many clients carry guilt rooted in unrealistic expectations, inherited beliefs, or circumstances beyond their control.

Reflective journaling allows clients to externalise guilt, examine its origins, and distinguish responsibility from self-punishment. Introducing higher-conscious perspectives—such as compassion, context, and impermanence—helps clients see their experiences within a broader human frame. Over time, guilt softens into learning, and regret transforms into wisdom rather than self-blame.

Grief and Loss

Grief is not a problem to be solved but a process to be honoured. Whether the loss involves death, relationships, health, or identity, grief alters emotional rhythms and disrupts meaning.

Counselling provides a safe space for expression without pressure to "move on." Alongside this emotional holding, solution-focused routines gently reintroduce structure—daily anchors, small responsibilities, and meaningful rituals. These do not erase grief; they help the individual coexist with it while slowly rebuilding stability and purpose.

Across all these emotional challenges, the counsellor's task remains consistent: to listen deeply, regulate gently, and guide without force. When emotions are understood rather than suppressed, they lose their power to dominate behaviour and instead become pathways to growth and resilience.

11. Practical Exercises

Understanding emotions intellectually is only the first step. Emotional mastery develops through practice—small, consistent exercises that train awareness, regulation, and response. The following practices are simple yet powerful, suitable for counsellors, students, and individuals alike. When practised regularly, they gradually rewire emotional patterns at both psychological and biochemical levels.

Daily Emotional Mapping

At the end of each day, briefly note:

- The emotional trigger (what happened),
- The emotional reaction (what you felt),
- The intensity (mild, moderate, intense),
- The behavioural response (what you did or avoided).

Over time, this mapping reveals recurring patterns. Clients often discover that the same emotion appears in different situations, pointing toward deeper subconscious triggers. Awareness itself begins the process of change.

1. Mindful Pause Drill

When you notice a strong emotional reaction arising, pause for ten seconds. Focus on your breath—especially the exhalation. Silently label the emotion: *"This is fear," "This is anger," "This is sadness."*

Naming the emotion activates the reflective parts of the brain and reduces impulsive reactions. This brief pause creates space for choice.

2. CBT Reflection

Ask yourself three questions:

- *What thought just crossed my mind?*
- *Is this thought a fact or an assumption?*
- *What is a more balanced or realistic alternative?*

This exercise helps identify negative automatic thoughts and replace them with rational, compassionate interpretations, preventing emotions from escalating unnecessarily.

3. REBT Challenge

Identify rigid beliefs hidden beneath emotional distress—statements beginning with *"must," "should," or "always."*

For example: *"I must never fail," "People should always appreciate me."*

Challenge these beliefs by asking: *Is this belief logical? Is it helpful? Is it humane?*

As beliefs soften, emotional intensity reduces.

4. Visualization Exercise

Close your eyes and recall a moment when you felt confident, calm, or deeply supported. Engage all senses—sight, sound, sensation. Stay with the memory for one to two minutes.

This practice stimulates beneficial biochemical patterns associated with safety and competence, counterbalancing stress responses.

5. Empathy Practice

In emotionally charged interactions, practise reflecting before responding. Silently ask:

What might this person be feeling beneath their words?

Respond by acknowledging emotion first, not logic: *"I can see this is stressful for you."*

This reduces conflict and strengthens relational intelligence.

6. Solution-Focused Mini-Goal

Instead of trying to solve the entire problem, identify one small, actionable step you can take within the next 24 hours.

Progress builds confidence, and confidence calms emotions. Small steps prevent emotional paralysis.

7. Assessment Integration

If you have completed any emotional intelligence or self-report assessments, revisit the results periodically. Choose one area to practise intentionally each week—such as impulse control, empathy, or emotional awareness—and observe real-life changes.

8. Collective Biochemical Pattern Exercise

Spend a few moments daily recalling experiences of connection—family support, teamwork, shared success, or collective resilience.

This reinforces the body's memory of safety within relationships, strengthening emotional balance and immune resilience. Many clients report reduced anxiety and improved clarity through this simple yet profound exercise.

Key Takeaways

1. Awareness of dual brain pathways allows conscious emotional control.
2. The limbic system triggers automatic reactions; the prefrontal cortex enables measured responses.
3. Behavioural patterns arise from subconscious and paraconscious triggers.
4. Emotional intelligence develops self-regulation, empathy, and social skills.
5. Visualization activates beneficial biochemical patterns.
6. EI improves relationships, productivity, and decision-making.
7. Solution-focused strategies foster incremental change.
8. Daily practice strengthens emotional mastery.

CHAPTER 4

THE ART AND SCIENCE OF COUNSELLING

Counselling is both an art and a science. Over my experience spanning more than five decades, I have observed that effective counselling emerges from a careful blending of human sensitivity, scientific understanding, ethical integrity, and practical wisdom. Techniques alone do not heal. Nor does empathy alone suffice. It is their integration—applied with discernment—that creates transformation.

Every client carries a unique story. No two journeys are identical. Yet beneath the surface diversity of problems—anxiety, anger, confusion, grief—lie common human patterns shaped by memory, emotion, and meaning. Each interaction, therefore, becomes more than a session. It becomes an opportunity to restore clarity where there is confusion, steadiness where there is fear, and agency where there once felt only reaction.

One such case that remains vivid in my memory was that of a young professional who sought help for persistent anxiety. At first glance, her concerns appeared ordinary—delayed emails from colleagues, minor misunderstandings at work, restless nights before presentations. Nothing dramatic. Nothing extraordinary.

Yet the intensity of her emotional responses told another story.

As she spoke, it became evident that beneath these everyday irritations lay a deeper pattern: a long-standing fear of failure shaped by childhood experiences in which mistakes had been met not with reassurance, but with criticism. What appeared to be present-day workplace stress was, in truth, an echo of earlier emotional conditioning.

Her words described the present.
Her body carried the past.

Each time she perceived disapproval, her breathing shortened. Her shoulders tightened. A brief silence in a meeting felt like rejection. A minor correction felt like humiliation. Her emotional–biochemical system reacted instantly—activating defensive alertness long before rational thought could intervene.

The science of counselling helped me understand what was happening. The art of counselling helped her see it for herself.

Through attentive observation, active listening, and reflective questioning, the layers gradually unfolded. Rather than analysing or correcting her immediately, I invited her to observe her own reactions—almost as if watching a recording of her behaviour. Slowly, she began to recognise how minor feedback felt like personal invalidation, how neutral events triggered disproportionate distress.

With this awareness came a subtle yet powerful shift.

The next time anxiety rose within her, she noticed it sooner—at the level of breath, muscle tension, and internal dialogue. That early recognition interrupted the familiar biochemical cascade before it gathered full force. Her breathing steadied. Her posture softened. Clarity returned.

And in that slowing, she discovered something transformative: choice.

What once felt automatic became conscious.
What once felt overwhelming became manageable.

This is where art and science meet.

Science explains the pathways—how emotional memory influences perception, how physiology mirrors fear, how cognition can regulate reaction. Art ensures that this understanding is delivered with compassion, timing, and trust.

Counselling, therefore, is not confined to a therapy room. Its principles travel wherever human beings interact—into corporate boardrooms, family conversations, leadership challenges, and moments of personal doubt. Wherever emotion shapes behaviour, counselling wisdom has relevance.

At its heart, counselling is the disciplined practice of helping another human being see clearly—so that they may respond wisely rather than react unconsciously.

And when clarity replaces confusion, transformation is no longer dramatic. It becomes natural.

Understanding Counselling

Counselling vs. Advice vs. Therapy *(Practitioner Perspective)*
Counselling is a collaborative and professional relationship in which the counsellor facilitates self-exploration, insight, and growth. While the theoretical distinctions between counselling, advice, and therapy were discussed earlier in this book, here we revisit them from a practical, field-based perspective.

In real practice, clients often arrive expecting direct solutions. Advice may offer short-term comfort, but it rarely creates inner transformation. Medical therapy, particularly in psychiatric contexts, focuses on diagnosis and symptom management, often supported by medication.

Counselling works differently. It invites clients to discover their own answers. As counsellors, we do not impose solutions—we create conditions for insight. Through reflective questioning, emotional processing, and structured techniques, clients learn to observe their own patterns and take responsibility for change.

Psychotherapy methods such as CBT, REBT, PCT, and SFBT are not merely theories—they are tools in the counsellor's hands:

- CBT helps clients track and restructure thinking patterns.
- REBT challenges rigid belief systems that generate distress.
- PCT builds healing through empathy and unconditional acceptance.
- SFBT focuses attention on possibilities and practical steps forward.

In practice, an effective counsellor integrates these approaches based on the client's needs, emotional readiness, and context. This flexibility transforms theory into healing action.

Overcoming Stigma *(Counsellor's Role)*

While stigma around counselling has been discussed earlier, here we explore how counsellors actively reduce stigma during sessions.

In real practice, fear of judgment may appear subtly - missed appointments, hesitation, or minimizing struggles. As professionals, we normalize emotional challenges and reframe counselling as mental fitness and self-leadership.

From my experience:

- Clients relax when counselling is presented as growth, not illness.
- Professionals respond positively when sessions are framed as leadership coaching.
- Students open up when counselling is positioned as skill-building.

Language matters:

"You are not broken. You are learning."
"This is emotional training, not treatment."

This subtle shift dissolves shame and builds motivation. The counsellor becomes not a "fixer," but a guide for inner mastery.

The Layers of Mind *(Applied Perspective)*

Earlier chapters explained the five layers of mind. Here, we explore how counsellors practically work with these layers.

Indian psychology identifies:

1. Conscious Mind – Current awareness
2. Subconscious Mind – Stored emotional patterns
3. Para-conscious Mind – Intuition and emerging insight
4. Universal Conscious – Collective human experience
5. Supreme Conscious – Higher awareness and purpose

In sessions, clients initially speak from the conscious level. As trust builds, deeper layers emerge. A skilled counsellor:

- Listens for subconscious patterns in language
- Notices emotional shifts
- Uses reflective questions to access deeper awareness

Example:
A corporate leader repeatedly expressed anger at team delays. Through dialogue, we uncovered subconscious fears of being judged as incompetent. Awareness allowed him to consciously alter his leadership style.

At universal levels, clients realize:

"I am not alone in this struggle."

At supreme levels, they experience:

- forgiveness
- acceptance
- purpose-driven decisions

Counsellors do not *teach* these layers—

They guide clients to experience them.

Building the Counsellor–Client Relationship

At the heart of all effective counselling lies the therapeutic relationship. Techniques matter, theories guide, but it is the quality of the human connection that determines whether healing can truly begin. Over decades of practice, I have seen that clients rarely remember the exact words spoken, but they never forget how safe, respected, and understood they felt.

A strong therapeutic alliance is built on a careful balance—empathy without over-identification, patience without passivity, and structure without rigidity. The counsellor walks beside the client, neither pulling them forward nor lagging behind, while remaining attentive to what is spoken and what remains unspoken.

Non-Verbal Communication

Much of counselling happens beyond words. Subtle gestures, posture, breathing patterns, and facial expressions often reveal emotional truths that language conceals. A client may say, "I'm fine," while their hands tremble, their shoulders tighten, or their eyes avoid contact.

Attentive observation allows the counsellor to sense these discrepancies without confrontation. A gentle reflection - *"As you say that, I notice your hands tightening"*—can open doors the intellect alone cannot. Non-verbal awareness deepens understanding and signals to the client that they are being seen as a whole person, not merely heard.

The Attitude Behind the Skills

Techniques are only as effective as the attitude that carries them. Authenticity, unconditional positive regard, and genuine curiosity form the invisible foundation of counselling. Clients intuitively sense when a counsellor is present versus merely performing a role.

When a counsellor approaches the client not as a problem to be fixed, but as a person to be understood, resistance softens. Safety emerges. Trust grows. In such an atmosphere, clients feel permitted to explore vulnerable emotions without fear of judgment or correction.

The Power of Silence in Counselling

Indian wisdom has long recognised the power of silence—not as emptiness, but as a living presence. In the *Brihadaranyaka Upanishad*, one of the most ancient philosophical texts of India, the sage Yājñavalkya is asked profound questions about the nature of reality and the self. On certain occasions, he does not respond with elaborate explanation. Instead, he remains silent.

To the modern reader, this may appear evasive. But within the Upanishadic tradition, silence was never ignorance. It was trust. Trust that truth cannot always be delivered through words—that it must arise within the seeker. The teacher's silence was not absence; it was an invitation. It created a space in which understanding could dawn from within rather than be imposed from outside.

Counselling, at its finest, mirrors this ancient insight.

Silence in counselling is not a gap to be filled. It is a space to be held.

I remember a young man who came to me after the sudden loss of his father. He spoke for several minutes—about hospital corridors, unfinished conversations, and the shock of absence. Then he stopped. His voice broke. His eyes filled. Words would not come.

I did not rush to reassure him.
I did not offer advice.
I did not attempt to explain grief.

I simply remained present.

The room was quiet, but not empty. It was full of shared humanity. After some time, he whispered,
"No one has let me cry like this."

That silence had done what language could not. It had given permission.

When silence is held with warmth—through a steady gaze, relaxed posture, and calm breath—it communicates something powerful:
"I am here. You are safe. Take your time."

From a psychological perspective, such silence allows the nervous system to regulate. The amygdala, which activates under perceived threat, begins to quiet. The prefrontal cortex regains influence. Emotional processing unfolds naturally. Insight ripens.

Yet silence must be understood correctly. It is not withdrawal. It is not indifference. And it cannot be used mechanically.

Early in my career, I learnt this through experience.

A young woman came to me after a painful breakup. She spoke briefly, then fell silent. I waited, remembering what I had been taught about "therapeutic silence." But something in the room felt tense.

Her eyes did not soften.
Her breathing did not slow.
Instead, her shoulders stiffened.

The silence stretched.

Finally, she looked at me and asked,
"Are you judging me too?"

In that moment, I realised my silence had not been experienced as supportive. It had felt distant.

I had remained quiet—but I had not communicated presence.

There is a profound difference.

I gently replied,
"No. I'm here with you. I'm trying to understand what this has been like."

Her posture changed almost immediately. The silence that followed was different—warmer, safer. This time, she continued speaking—not about betrayal, but about shame and fear of being unworthy of love.

That session reshaped my understanding. Silence heals only when it carries empathy.

Indian philosophical traditions never describe silence as emptiness. In the Upanishadic model, the teacher's quietude is infused with awareness. The seeker does not feel abandoned; they feel supported in discovering truth within themselves.

Similarly, in counselling, silence must carry subtle signals:

A softened expression.
Attentive stillness.
Unhurried breathing.
An atmosphere that conveys, without words, "You are not alone here."

When silence is held with attunement, emotions surface safely. When offered without warmth, it may be perceived as rejection.

Silence, therefore, is not the absence of intervention.
It is a refined form of intervention.

It is the counsellor's willingness to resist the impulse to correct, interpret, or impress—trusting that insight often ripens in stillness.

As I often tell young counsellors:

"If you speak too soon, you may answer the wrong question.
If you wait with care, the real question will reveal itself."

And when it does, healing reaches a depth that words alone rarely touch.

Counselling Approaches in Action

If silence represents the art of counselling, structured approaches represent its science.

Presence opens the door. Method provides direction.

While the therapeutic relationship forms the living foundation of healing, structured approaches offer clarity and movement. Each therapeutic model provides a different lens through which human experience can be understood. A skilled counsellor does not cling rigidly to one framework. Instead, methods are chosen and integrated flexibly—guided not by preference, but by the client's unique need in that moment.

Just as a physician selects medicine based on diagnosis, the counsellor selects approach based on emotional patterns, cognitive habits, personality structure, and situational demands.

Let us see how these approaches come alive in practice.

1. Cognitive Behavioural Therapy (CBT)

A client struggling with procrastination may not lack intelligence or ability. Often, what blocks action is an automatic thought quietly repeating in the background:

"I'll never succeed."
"There's no point starting."
"I'll only embarrass myself."

These thoughts feel true because they are familiar.

Through CBT, the client begins to identify these distortions—not as facts, but as interpretations. Instead of immediately replacing them, we first observe them. When do they arise? What emotion follows? What behaviour results?

By tracking thoughts, emotions, and actions daily, patterns become visible. Avoidance is no longer mysterious. It becomes understandable.

As awareness increases, distorted thoughts are gently questioned:

"Is it true that you will never succeed?"
"What evidence supports that belief?"
"Have there been times you completed something successfully?"

Gradually, avoidance gives way to constructive engagement. Behaviour shifts—not through force, but through clarity.

CBT teaches the client that thoughts are powerful—but not always accurate.

2. Rational Emotive Behaviour Therapy (REBT)

An executive overwhelmed by performance pressure may carry an even more rigid internal belief:

"If I fail, my career is finished."
"I must always perform perfectly."
"Mistakes are unacceptable."

Notice the language—*must*, *always*, *finished*.

REBT focuses on identifying these absolutist beliefs and examining their logic. Together, we explore:

Is it realistic to never fail?
Does one mistake truly erase an entire career?
Who defined this standard of perfection?

As the client begins to see the exaggeration within their own thinking, something softens. The fear does not disappear overnight, but its intensity reduces.

Replacing rigid demands with humane perspectives—"I prefer to succeed, but I can tolerate setbacks"—transforms emotional distress into manageable concern.

REBT reminds us that suffering often lies not in events themselves, but in the rigid meanings we attach to them.

3. Person-Centered Therapy (PCT)

A teenager facing social anxiety may not need immediate cognitive restructuring. They may not yet be ready to challenge thoughts.

What they need first is acceptance.

In such moments, solutions are secondary. Safety is primary.

Through empathy, warmth, and unconditional positive regard, the counsellor reflects feelings gently:

"It sounds like you feel invisible in class."
"You worry that others are judging you."
"That must feel exhausting."
No correction.
No premature reassurance.
Only understanding.

In this atmosphere of non-judgment, the adolescent begins to explore fears openly. Shame reduces. Self-acceptance grows. And as acceptance deepens, confidence begins to emerge naturally.

PCT reminds us that healing often begins not with advice, but with being fully seen.

4. Solution-Focused Brief Therapy (SFBT)

A manager caught in team conflict may feel trapped in endless analysis—who said what, who started it, who is at fault.

SFBT gently shifts the lens.

Instead of asking, "Why is this happening?" we ask:

"If this issue were resolved tomorrow, what would be the first small sign you would notice?"
"What would be different in your tone? In the team's behaviour?"

The focus moves from problem to possibility.

As the client describes a preferred future, small, achievable steps begin to surface. Perhaps one conversation needs to happen. Perhaps one acknowledgment needs to be offered.

Action restores momentum.

SFBT demonstrates that clarity about where we want to go often reduces the weight of where we are.

In practice, these approaches rarely operate in isolation. A counsellor may begin with person-centered empathy, introduce CBT clarity, soften rigid beliefs through REBT, and move toward SFBT action—all within the arc of a therapeutic journey.

Presence creates safety.
Insight creates understanding.
Structure creates movement.

When art and science meet, counselling becomes not merely conversation—but transformation.

Challenges in Counselling

If counselling were only about techniques, it would be simple.
But counselling is about human beings. And where there are human beings, there are complexities.

Even the most experienced counsellors encounter moments of uncertainty, resistance, emotional strain, and cultural misunderstanding. These challenges are not signs of failure. They are inherent to the depth of the work.

Awareness of them protects both practitioner and client.

Client Resistance: Protection, Not Opposition

Not every client walks in ready to speak their deepest truth.

Some circle around the pain.
Some intellectualise.
Some joke.
Some change the topic at the very moment insight begins to emerge.

To the untrained eye, this may look like avoidance or lack of cooperation. But resistance is rarely rebellion. It is protection.

The subconscious mind guards wounds carefully. It tests the room. It tests the counsellor. It asks silently:

"Is it safe here?"

I recall a client who spent three sessions discussing workplace politics in elaborate detail. Only later did it emerge that beneath the frustration lay a childhood memory of humiliation by a teacher. The present was easier to speak about than the past.

If I had forced the deeper issue prematurely, trust would have fractured.

Instead, gentle reflection and respectful questioning created space:

"I notice this situation seems to affect you more deeply than others. What does it remind you of?"

Silence. A pause. Then a shift.

Healing unfolds at the client's pace—not the counsellor's.

Resistance, when respected, becomes a doorway.

Emotional Contagion: The Counsellor's Inner Discipline

Counselling requires empathy—but empathy carries weight.

When a client speaks of grief, the counsellor feels its echo.
When a client describes rage, the room itself tightens.
When despair is voiced repeatedly, it lingers.

This natural resonance is sometimes called emotional contagion. It is not weakness. It is human attunement.

Yet without awareness, this resonance can accumulate. The counsellor may carry fragments of clients' sorrow home. Irritability may rise unexpectedly. Fatigue may deepen.

In such moments, technique alone is insufficient. Inner discipline becomes essential.

Mindfulness practices—brief pauses between sessions, conscious breathing, grounding rituals—help the counsellor release what does not belong to them. Supervision provides a mirror when blind spots form. Regular self-care restores equilibrium.

Empathy must be balanced with boundaries.

The goal is not emotional detachment—but regulated presence:
feeling with the client, without being consumed by the feeling.

Cultural Sensitivity: Honour Before Intervention

No client arrives as a blank slate.

Each carries a world—language, family structure, spiritual beliefs, social expectations, gender roles, community norms. These factors shape how distress is expressed and how help is received.

In one family, emotional openness may be encouraged.
In another, silence may signify strength.
In one culture, direct eye contact conveys confidence.
In another, it may appear disrespectful.

Without cultural sensitivity, misunderstanding grows quietly.

I once worked with a young man who rarely made eye contact. Initially, a less aware observer might have interpreted this as evasiveness. In reality, he had been raised to lower his gaze in the presence of elders as a sign of respect. What seemed like withdrawal was reverence.

Counselling becomes effective not when it imposes interpretation, but when it honours context.

To ask, "What does this mean in your family?"
To ask, "How is this usually handled in your community?"
These questions prevent assumptions and strengthen rapport.

Cultural humility is not optional. It is ethical responsibility.

The Deeper Challenge

Beneath resistance, emotional contagion, and cultural complexity lies a deeper challenge: the counsellor must remain steady amidst uncertainty.

Not every session produces breakthrough.
Not every insight leads to immediate change.
Not every story resolves neatly.

The art of counselling lies in remaining present—even when clarity is delayed.

When challenges are met with awareness rather than frustration, they do not weaken the process. They refine it.

For in counselling, as in life, growth often occurs not in smooth moments—but in the careful navigation of difficulty.

From Challenge to Mastery

If counselling teaches us anything, it is humility.

No technique works without trust.
No insight penetrates without safety.
No transformation endures without ethical grounding.

The challenges we encounter—resistance, emotional contagion, cultural complexity—are not interruptions to the counselling process. They are part of it. They refine the counsellor's awareness. They deepen patience. They remind us that counselling is not mechanical problem-solving; it is a living exchange between two human nervous systems, two histories, two inner worlds.

And it is precisely here—where science meets sensitivity—that counselling reveals itself fully as both art and discipline.

The science provides structure.
The art provides attunement.

A counsellor may understand cognitive restructuring, trauma pathways, or behavioural reinforcement. Yet without emotional presence, these remain tools without touch. Conversely, warmth without structure can become directionless empathy.

Mastery lies in integration.

It lies in sensing when to question and when to remain silent.
When to introduce structure and when to allow unfolding.
When to gently challenge and when to simply hold space.

Over the years, I have observed that the most transformative sessions are rarely the most technical. They are the ones where the client feels deeply seen—and where structured guidance is offered without overpowering their autonomy.

Counselling, then, becomes a dynamic balance:

- Insight without intrusion
- Empathy without enmeshment
- Structure without rigidity
- Compassion without overextension

And when this balance is maintained, something remarkable happens.

Clients begin to internalise the process.

They start pausing before reacting.
They start questioning their automatic thoughts.
They begin holding silence within themselves.

In time, they no longer need the counsellor in the same way. The external guide becomes an internal voice of steadiness.

That is the true art and science of counselling:
not dependence—but self-regulation.

Not advice—but awakening.

And with that foundation established, we are ready to move deeper—into the refined skills, ethical clarity, and integrative approaches that allow counselling to operate safely, responsibly, and powerfully across diverse contexts.

Practical Exercises

Regular practice of the following exercises will help readers—whether ordinary individuals or professional counsellors—develop competence, confidence, and deeper insight.

1. Active Empathic Listening

- Focus fully on the speaker without interrupting.
- Observe not only words but emotions behind them.
- Reflect feelings by saying, *"I sense you're feeling…"*
- Avoid judgment, advice, or quick solutions.

Purpose: Builds trust and emotional safety.

2. Thought Mapping (CBT / REBT Technique)

- Write down a recent stressful situation.
- Identify the automatic thought (e.g., *"I always fail."*)
- Question its truth.
- Replace it with a rational alternative.

Purpose: Restructures negative thinking.

3. Solution-Focused "Miracle Question"

This technique shifts focus from problems to solutions.

How to practise:

Ask:
"Suppose tonight, while you are asleep, a miracle happens and your problem is completely solved. When you wake up tomorrow, what will be the first small sign that tells you things are better?"

Encourage detail:

- What would you do differently?
- How would others notice?
- What would you feel inside?

Identify one small action you can take today to move toward this future.
Purpose: Builds hope and actionable direction.

4. Non-Verbal Awareness

- Observe posture, tone, facial expressions.
- Adjust for openness and warmth.

Purpose: Enhances emotional attunement.

5. Daily Reflection Journal

- Write one meaningful interaction daily.
- Note your emotional response.
- Identify lessons learned.

Purpose: Builds continuous self-awareness.

Accessing Layers of Mind

Guided reflection integrates conscious, subconscious, para-conscious, universal, and supreme levels. This helps clients recognize patterns and make intentional choices.

Key Takeaways

- Counselling is both an art (presence, empathy, silence) and a science (structured methods like CBT, REBT, PCT, SFBT).
- Non-verbal communication—eye contact, posture, silence—often speaks louder than words.
- Attitude behind techniques matters more than tools.
- Silence enables deep processing.
- Integrative approaches create flexibility.
- Informed consent builds trust.

CHAPTER 5

ADVANCED COUNSELLING TECHNIQUES AND ETHICAL PRACTICE

The Living Room of Counselling

Every counsellor remembers those moments that change not only the client but also the counsellor. Advanced counselling is not about using a "complicated tool"; it is about being fully present at those delicate turning points where a human being decides whether to despair or to hope, whether to break or to heal.

I will never forget one late evening during the peak of the Covid pandemic. My phone rang, and on the other end was Ravi, a middle-aged businessman who had lost both parents in the span of just two weeks. His voice was hollow, his breathing uneven. He said in a trembling whisper, "I don't even know why I should live anymore."

In that moment, all my years of training and decades of practice were tested. No manual could dictate what to say. No technique could be applied mechanically. What mattered was my ability to hold the silence, as we have explored earlier about the power of presence, to make Ravi feel that even in his unbearable pain, he was not alone.

I spoke softly:

"Ravi, right now, you don't need answers. You need someone to carry this heaviness with you. Let us breathe together, one breath at a time."

For several minutes, we did nothing but breathe. Gradually, his sobbing slowed, his words became clearer, and space was created for him to express the storm inside. That session was not about "solving" grief—it was about creating a safe container where his grief could be expressed without fear, without judgment, without breaking him further.

This is the essence of advanced counselling: being skilful, ethical, and deeply human when life tests the limits of ordinary words.

Why Advanced Techniques Matter

Advanced counselling techniques are not a luxury for the experienced practitioner—they are a necessity. Basic empathy and listening, as discussed in earlier chapters, are invaluable, but when you sit with someone whose trauma has shattered their sense of safety, or whose anxiety grips their body like a vice, you need something more.

You need techniques that can reach beneath the surface—to the subconscious where memories lie, to the para-conscious where fears brew, and to the universal consciousness where healing symbols and meanings reside. Yet, these techniques are never applied like a formula. They are always guided by ethics, respect, and the counsellor's own inner clarity.

Carl Rogers once said, "The curious paradox is that when I accept myself just as I am, then I can change." This truth applies not only to clients but to counsellors as well. The paradox of advanced counselling is that we use structured methods, but the magic often lies in the unstructured—our presence, our silence, our capacity to accept the client fully.

A Glimpse into Trauma Work

Consider the case of Divya, a young woman who came to me after a terrible car accident. Months had passed, but every time she heard the screech of brakes, her body froze in terror. Her friends told her to "forget it," her relatives said, "move on," but her nervous system had not moved on. Her amygdala—the brain's alarm system we discussed earlier—still treated every screech as if death was moments away.

With Divya, I did not begin by telling her to "be strong." Instead, we entered the memory carefully, step by step, using guided imagery. I asked her to describe the accident, not in one flood of terror, but in fragments, pausing whenever her body stiffened. At each pause, I grounded her in the present—reminding her of her safety, her strength, and her survival. Slowly, we rewove the memory from being a prison into being a chapter of her story. Months later, she told me, "Now when I hear brakes, I don't freeze. I know I'm safe."

This is advanced counselling—not erasing the past but transforming the relationship with it.

Ethics at the Heart

Whenever we enter such deep waters, ethics is not just important—it is everything. Without ethical clarity, advanced techniques can become manipulation; with it, they become healing.

I once counselled a young man who had been sent by his family. They wanted him to "change" certain aspects of his personality they disapproved of. Here, my role was not to become an instrument of family pressure. My responsibility was to him, not to the expectations imposed upon him. We worked on his self-image, his aspirations, his emotional health—not on moulding him into someone else's design.

This is the sacred boundary of counselling. We do not own our clients; we serve them. We do not impose; we invite. We do not manipulate; we guide. And when medical intervention is required—when the pain crosses into psychiatric territory—our duty is to refer, not to pretend we can do everything. That humility is not a weakness; it is professionalism.

The Colours of Culture

Advanced counselling is not merely about technique—it is about attunement. It means meeting people where they are, not where we expect them to be. Culture is not a decorative backdrop to a person's life; it shapes their fears, their hopes, their language of suffering, and even their imagination of healing.

During the pandemic, I often witnessed how deeply cultural context influenced the way people processed grief and uncertainty. When I spoke with Indian clients, I found that philosophical and spiritual references did not feel abstract—they felt familiar, grounding. A grieving father once told me he could not understand why life had taken his son. His anger was directed not only at fate, but at himself. In our conversation, I gently recalled a verse from the *Bhagavad Gita*: *"Yoga⊠ karmasu kauśalam"* (Chapter 2, Verse 50), translated by S. Radhakrishnan (1948) as "Yoga is skill in action."

I did not quote it as doctrine. I invited reflection.
"If yoga is skill in action," I asked him softly, "could living through this pain with dignity also be a form of yoga?"
There was a long silence. Then he said, slowly,
"If skill in living through suffering is yoga, then perhaps I can honour my son by living well."

That shift did not remove his grief. But it gave it direction. It reframed endurance not as helplessness, but as sacred effort.

When counselling international clients, however, I rarely drew upon scriptural language. Not because the wisdom was absent, but because the doorway was different. A verse that resonates deeply in one culture may feel distant in another. What heals is not the quotation itself, but the meaning it carries.

With many clients from Western contexts, I framed similar insights through psychological language—drawing, for instance, upon Daniel Goleman's model of Emotional Intelligence. We would explore self-awareness as the ability to notice emotional activation, self-regulation as the capacity to pause before reacting, and resilience as the disciplined return to balance after disruption.

In one session, a senior professional from Europe described his frustration in purely cognitive terms. "I know my reactions are exaggerated," he said. "I just can't seem to stop them." Instead of invoking philosophical reflection, we mapped his responses using the language of neural pathways and emotional conditioning. We examined how repeated stress responses strengthen certain circuits in the brain—and how intentional pauses can gradually reshape them.

As he understood this scientifically, something shifted. The explanation felt rational. Accessible. Grounded.

The insight was fundamentally the same as the grieving father's: awareness creates choice. But the language was tuned differently.

The wisdom was universal.
The expression was cultural.

This is the essence of advanced counselling: flexibility without dilution. Just as a river does not lose its source when it bends around mountains or widens across plains, counselling does not lose its integrity when it adapts to belief systems, education, or worldview. It simply flows in a form the client can receive—without forcing them to translate what already feels foreign.

Techniques That Touch the Depths

There are moments in counselling when conversation reaches a subtle boundary. The client understands. They articulate their patterns with clarity. They may even analyse their own behaviour with impressive precision. Yet something remains unmoved.

The conscious mind agrees.
The deeper layers remain guarded.

In such moments, repeating explanation becomes counterproductive. Insight without experience rarely transforms behaviour. It is here that advanced techniques become necessary—not as dramatic interventions, but as carefully guided invitations inward.

These methods are neither mystical nor manipulative. They are disciplined approaches refined through years of clinical observation and ethical practice. Their purpose is not to overpower resistance, but to respect it—to move gently around the defences the mind has constructed for protection.

At this depth, healing is no longer merely cognitive. It becomes experiential—and therefore biochemical.

When an old memory is revisited with fear, the body reproduces the same stress chemistry it once encoded. Muscles tighten. Breath shortens. Cortisol rises. The past is not only remembered; it is physiologically reactivated through what I have earlier described as the Collective Biochemical Messenger System—the intricate network of neurotransmitters, hormones, neuropeptides, and immune signals that carry the signature of our emotional states.

But here lies the therapeutic opportunity.

If a memory can reactivate distress chemistry, it can also—when approached differently—reshape it.

Sometimes this involves guided imagery. By revisiting formative experiences within a structured and safe framework, clients can encounter old memories without being overwhelmed by them. The past is not relived—it is re-encountered with greater awareness and emotional support. As the emotional meaning shifts, so too does the biochemical pattern associated with it.

At other times, therapeutic meditation allows breath and attention to calm the autonomic nervous system. When the body shifts from sympathetic activation (fight–flight) toward parasympathetic regulation (rest–restore), a different constellation of biochemical messengers begins to circulate—those associated with safety, bonding, and stability. The mind becomes more receptive because the body is no longer braced for threat.

And sometimes the work is narrative. A client may see their life only through the lens of failure. By reframing the story—not denying pain, but recognising resilience—the emotional tone changes. That change is not abstract; it is embodied. Posture softens. Voice steadies. The internal chemical climate reorganises.

I recall a woman who repeatedly told me,
"I know my fear is irrational, but I can't stop feeling it."
Her words were logical.
Her nervous system was not.

Rather than debating the irrationality of her fear, I invited her into a brief imagery exercise. I asked her to visualise the earliest moment she remembered feeling that same tightening in her chest.

She described a classroom. She was ten years old. A teacher had criticised her publicly. The humiliation had lodged somewhere deep.

As she narrated the scene, her breathing altered. Her shoulders drew inward. The emotional–biochemical imprint of that childhood moment resurfaced in real time.

In that moment, the issue was no longer "irrational fear."
It was an unintegrated emotional memory reactivating its original biochemical signature.

I gently asked her to imagine sitting beside that younger version of herself—not as a critic, but as a compassionate adult. To offer reassurance that had not been available then.

As she did, her breath gradually lengthened. Her facial tension eased. Tears came—not of panic, but of release.

The biochemical pattern shifted.

The fear did not vanish instantly. But its intensity diminished. Over subsequent sessions, the once-automatic surge of anxiety lost its force. The old messenger system had been gently recalibrated through new emotional meaning.

Advanced counselling, then, is not about implanting new ideas. It is about reorganising emotional memory—so that the body no longer reacts to yesterday as though it were today.

It works not only at the level of thought,
but at the level of lived, embodied experience.

And when the emotional–biochemical climate changes, behaviour follows naturally.

The client begins to experience themselves not as broken,
but as adaptive—capable of reshaping even deeply encoded patterns.
That is not suggestion.
It is neurobiological possibility aligned with compassionate presence.

Narrative Therapy: Healing Through Stories

Human beings are storytellers. Long before psychology became a discipline, we made meaning of joy and suffering through narrative. We remember through stories. We transmit identity through stories. We interpret our past and imagine our future through the language we repeatedly use about ourselves.

Yet sometimes, the story a person tells about themselves becomes a prison rather than a path.

I recall counselling a schoolteacher, Mala, who described herself consistently as a "failure." Her marriage had ended painfully. Her health had declined under prolonged stress. She felt diminished in the eyes of society and in her own estimation.

Every sentence she spoke carried the same undertone:

"I always ruin things."
"I can never manage."
"My life is finished."
Notice the absolutes—*always*, *never*, *finished.*
Her narrative was no longer describing events; it was defining identity.

As she repeated this story, her body reflected it. Her shoulders curved inward. Her breath shortened. Her tone flattened. The narrative was not merely cognitive—it was embodied. Each repetition reactivated the same emotional–biochemical pattern, strengthening neural pathways associated with shame, defeat, and helplessness.

Modern trauma research shows that memory is not a static recording but a living process. Each time a painful memory is recalled, it becomes temporarily malleable before being stored again—a process known as memory reconsolidation. If the recall occurs in the same emotional state, the pattern strengthens. If it occurs within safety, reflection, and new meaning, the emotional charge can soften.

This is where narrative therapy becomes transformative.

Developed and articulated by Michael White and David Epston, narrative therapy proposes that "the person is not the problem; the problem is the problem." Identity is shaped not by events alone, but by the dominant story we construct around them. By externalising problems and exploring alternative narratives, individuals rediscover agency and forgotten strengths.

With Mala, we did not dispute the facts of her divorce or illness. Instead, we gently separated her identity from those experiences.

Instead of "I am a failure," we explored:
"You have experienced painful failures—but are you identical to them?"

At first, she hesitated. The old narrative felt solid, almost sacred in its certainty. But as we carefully retraced her life, other chapters surfaced.

She had supported her students during lockdown, calling those who were struggling.
She had endured social stigma yet continued functioning with dignity.
She cared for her aging mother every day, despite her own exhaustion.

These were not dramatic victories. They were quiet strengths—excluded from the dominant story because they did not fit the theme of failure.

Gradually, her language shifted.

From:
"I am a failure."
To:
"I have faced failures."
And later:
"I am a survivor."
"I am a teacher still learning."

In those moments, something deeper than language changed. The emotional tone accompanying her memories softened. Tears replaced tension. Her breathing deepened. The narrative was no longer encoded with shame alone; it began to integrate resilience.

This is the subtle power of narrative therapy. It does not erase pain. It does not deny reality. It reorganises meaning.

When a traumatic memory is revisited within safety and compassion, the brain stores it differently. The emotional–biochemical signature shifts. What was once fused with identity becomes contextualised as experience. The wound remains part of the story—but no longer the author of it.

And this is where the deepest impact occurs.

Advanced counselling does not impose optimism. It invites authorship.

It helps a person move from being a passive character trapped inside a painful script to becoming an active narrator capable of revision.

When the story expands, the self expands.
When identity softens, physiology follows.
When meaning shifts, vitality returns.

A human life is never a single chapter.

Narrative therapy reminds us—gently but powerfully—that no matter how dark a page may appear, it is never the final sentence.

Mindfulness and Presence: Returning to the Now

If narrative therapy reshapes the story of the past, mindfulness restores the ground beneath the present.

Many clients do not suffer only from events—they suffer from time. Their minds wander endlessly: replaying yesterday's regrets, rehearsing tomorrow's catastrophes. The body remains here, but the mind lives elsewhere. When this split persists, distress deepens.

Mindfulness-based counselling offers something profoundly simple: a return to now.

Not through denial of fear.
Not through suppression of thought.
But through steady awareness of experience as it unfolds.

During the pandemic, one young IT professional, Kabir, was consumed by anticipatory fear. His thoughts circled relentlessly:

"What if I die tomorrow?"
"What if my family dies?"
"What if I leave my daughter alone?"

These were not occasional worries. They were immersive mental rehearsals of catastrophe. Even in the absence of immediate danger, his body reacted as though threat were present. His breath shortened. Sleep fragmented. His muscles remained tense. His nervous system stayed in survival mode.

This is the power of unregulated imagination: the brain does not fully distinguish between real and vividly imagined threat. The emotional–biochemical system responds accordingly. Stress hormones surge. Defensive patterns consolidate.

Rather than arguing with his thoughts, we began somewhere deeper—the body.

I guided him gently:

"Feel the breath entering your lungs.
Notice the rise and fall of your chest.
Listen to the sound of your breath.
Right now, in this moment, what is happening?"

At first, his mind resisted. Thoughts pulled him away every few seconds—toward hospitals, news reports, imagined funerals. Each time, I invited him back without criticism:

"Notice that the mind has wandered.
Now return."

This returning is the practice.

In Indian philosophical language, this capacity resembles *pratyahara*—the gentle withdrawal of attention from external agitation back toward inner steadiness. It also echoes the ancient concept of *sakshi bhava*—the witnessing attitude—where one observes thoughts and emotions without becoming engulfed by them.

The witness does not fight the storm.
It simply sees it.

As Kabir practised, something subtle began to change. The pauses between anxious thoughts lengthened. His breathing deepened. His shoulders relaxed. The body, receiving repeated signals of safety, began recalibrating its internal chemistry. The stress-driven cascade softened. Calming biochemical messengers emerged more consistently.

Weeks later, he said quietly:

"For the first time in months, I sat with my daughter and listened to her laughter without fear."

Nothing external had changed. The pandemic continued. Uncertainty remained.

But his relationship with the present moment had transformed.

Mindfulness had not eliminated risk.
It had restored presence.

From a psychological perspective, mindfulness strengthens the observing self—the ability to experience thoughts without fusing with them. From a physiological perspective, repeated present-moment awareness stabilises the emotional–biochemical system, teaching the nervous system that not every thought demands a full survival response.

From a philosophical perspective, it reconnects the individual to a deeper stillness that is not destroyed by passing mental waves.

Mindfulness is often mistaken for withdrawal from life.

In truth, it is a disciplined return to it—one breath, one sensation, one sound at a time.

Advanced counselling does not merely interpret the mind.

It helps the person rediscover the steady ground within which all thoughts arise and pass.

And it is from that ground that true healing becomes possible.

Integrative Counselling: Meeting Clients Where They Are

Rarely does one technique resolve the complexity of a human life.

People do not suffer in single dimensions. Their distress may live simultaneously in memory, in thought patterns, in the body, in identity, and in relationship. To respond to such layered experience with a single rigid method is often insufficient.

This is where integrative counselling becomes essential.

Integrative counselling is not the careless mixing of techniques. It is the thoughtful blending of approaches—guided not by preference, but by the client's evolving needs. It requires clinical discernment, ethical clarity, and deep listening.

With Divya, the car accident survivor mentioned earlier, her trauma did not exist in one place alone.

It lived in her memory—in flashes of impact and sound.
It lived in her thoughts—"What if it happens again?"

It lived in her body—tightening muscles whenever she entered a vehicle.
And it lived in her sense of safety—a subtle loss of trust in the world.

To approach her healing, we worked layer by layer.

First, through guided imagery, we approached the traumatic memory gently—not to relive it recklessly, but to re-encounter it within safety. As she visualised the accident scene with structured guidance, her breathing was regulated. The memory, once chaotic and overwhelming, began to reorganise under conscious awareness.

Next, through Cognitive Behavioural Therapy, we examined the catastrophic beliefs that had grown around the event. "Every road is dangerous." "I will lose control." These thoughts were not dismissed—they were explored, questioned, and softened. Probability replaced exaggeration. Realistic assessment replaced fear-driven assumption.

At the same time, mindfulness practices grounded her in present sensation. When her body tensed in a moving car, she practised noticing the seat beneath her, the rhythm of breath, the steady movement of the vehicle. The present moment slowly began to override the past imprint.

Each technique addressed a different layer:

Imagery touched memory.
CBT addressed cognition.
Mindfulness regulated physiology.

Together, they recalibrated her emotional–biochemical system. The repeated pairing of safety with previously triggering stimuli allowed new patterns to form. What had once triggered a survival cascade gradually evoked steadiness.

Healing did not occur because one method was superior.

It occurred because the right methods were combined with sensitivity.

Over decades of practice, this integrative approach gradually deepened and refined itself. What began as the application of established models slowly evolved into a more fluid, presence-based way of working—one that moves between conscious dialogue, subconscious access, and mind–body regulation with deliberate care.

In later chapters, I will describe how these experiences shaped certain evolved techniques of my own—not as replacements for classical methods, but as extensions of them. They emerged from years of observing how memory, meaning, breath, and belief interact within what I call the Collective Biochemical Messenger System.

But at their core, these techniques are not innovations for their own sake.

They are simply the natural progression of integrative counselling—
where science, experience, and presence converge.

Textbooks provide frameworks.

Healing unfolds in living human complexity.

The art of integrative counselling lies not in mastering many tools—
but in knowing when to use each one, when to combine them,
and when simply to sit, steady and attentive,
allowing the next doorway to open on its own.

Ethical Compass in Deep Waters

Working with such techniques requires caution. The deeper we go into memory, imagination, or emotions, the greater the risk of misunderstanding. That is why informed consent is essential in advanced counselling.

Before starting deep work, I explain to clients what the process involves, what they may feel, and the possible risks. For example, when exploring subconscious memories, I caution:

"Sometimes, you may experience very vivid emotions or even memory-like impressions. These do not always mean they are literal memories. They may be products of imagination or emotional states. If such experiences occur, it is important to share them openly with me, so we can work through them safely."

This prevents what psychologists call false memory syndrome.

Informed Consent and Physical Touch

Ethics also extends to those rare moments in counselling where physical touch may be part of a relaxation or grounding exercise. For example, a counsellor might lightly place a hand on a client's shoulder to guide them in releasing muscular tension, or gently adjust their posture during a deep-breathing practice.

However, touch in counselling is extremely sensitive. What may feel natural and supportive to one client can feel invasive or uncomfortable to another. This is why explicit, informed consent is absolutely essential before any form of physical touch is used.

When I explain this to clients, I say something like:

"At certain points, if you are comfortable, I may guide you physically—such as helping you relax your shoulders. If you would rather, I not do that, please let me know. This is completely your choice."

Consent should always be documented in writing, ideally through a signed consent form. In cases where the client has a psychiatric illness, or when there are family concerns, it is advisable to also have the consent signed by accompanying family members. This protects both the client and the counsellor.

Such safeguards are not about bureaucracy; they are about preserving trust, dignity, and safety. In counselling, trust is the foundation. Without it, no advanced technique—however powerful—can truly help.

Family Involvement and Protection

Particularly in cases of psychiatric conditions, clients may not always be cooperative or may later misinterpret counselling experiences. I recall counselling a young man with severe mood swings. At times, he accused me of "not listening" even when the session was structured around his concerns. For his safety and mine, I ensured his family was briefed and present when appropriate, and that informed consent was signed by both client and family.

This is not bureaucracy—it is protection. It safeguards trust, prevents false accusations, and ensures that counselling remains a healing process rather than a contested one.

Culture, Symbolism, and Ethics

Advanced counselling also requires sensitivity to cultural and spiritual frameworks. Some clients connect deeply with spiritual imagery; others prefer scientific explanations. For example, a grieving widow once told me she found comfort in imagining her late husband's soul resting in peace. Here, my role was not to impose my beliefs but to support hers, as long as they aided healing.

In contrast, a corporate client abroad preferred to understand grief through the neurobiology of stress hormones and recovery pathways. Both approaches were equally valid, because both honoured the client's worldview.

Ethical practice is not about pushing one narrative but about respecting the client's cultural and personal meaning-making systems.

The Core Truth

Whether we use narrative therapy, mindfulness, integrative counselling, or other advanced methods, the heart of the work remains the same: respect the client, uphold ethics, and guide them with skill and compassion.

Techniques are like musical instruments. Some counsellors play the violin of CBT, others the flute of mindfulness, still others the drum of narrative therapy. But what matters is not the instrument—it is the music of healing, played with sincerity, clarity, and responsibility.

When Techniques Become Transformation

Advanced counselling is not about "showcasing" techniques—it is about using them with sensitivity so that a client's life can shift in real, tangible ways. Let me share three stories that illustrate how advanced approaches, when combined with presence and ethics, become transformative.

Case 1 – Healing a Mother's Guilt

Shalini, a young mother, came to me during the pandemic, carrying immense guilt. Her five-year-old son had contracted Covid, and though he recovered quickly, she said, "I failed as a mother. If I had been more careful, he would never have fallen sick."

No amount of reassurance from friends helped her. The guilt had settled deep into her subconscious. Through guided imagery, I asked her to recall a memory where she felt she had been a caring, protective mother. She remembered a night when her son had high fever years earlier, and how she stayed up caring for him until he slept peacefully.

As she described that scene, I said gently:

"That same mother—the one who cared so deeply—is the one who is here now. You have not failed. Illness does not erase your love."

Tears flowed, but the guilt began to soften. She later told me, "For the first time, I could forgive myself."

Here, advanced counselling was not about logic alone. It was about accessing subconscious patterns, reframing them through imagery, and guiding her towards self-compassion.

Case 2 – The Manager and His Temper

Raghav, a mid-level manager in a multinational company, came with a recurring issue: he often lost his temper during meetings. His words, though unintended, left team members demotivated.

We explored his triggers and found a subconscious pattern. As a child, he had been harshly criticized by his father whenever he made mistakes. Now, when his team erred, that old wound was reactivated.

We used a combination of CBT and mindfulness. Raghav learned to identify the surge of irritation as an "amygdala signal," not as an unavoidable truth. By pausing, breathing, and reframing thoughts—"They are learning, not failing me"—he gradually gained control.

Months later, one of his team members told him, "Earlier we feared your reactions. Now, we feel encouraged to learn." That feedback was more than progress; it was transformation.

Case 3 – Grief into Purpose

During my telephonic Covid counselling, I worked with Arun, who had lost his younger brother to the virus. He said bitterly, "What's the use of anything? Life is meaningless."

For weeks, we held space for his grief. Then, using elements of solution-focused therapy, I asked, "If your brother could see you today, what would he want for you?"

Arun was silent, then whispered, "He would want me to take care of our parents."

That small realization became his anchor. From despair, he found purpose. Later, he began volunteering to support Covid-affected families. He said, "I still miss my brother every day. But now I live in a way that honours him."

This is the power of advanced counselling—not to erase grief, but to help clients transform pain into meaning.

Reflections for the Reader

Dear reader, as you journey through these stories, remember that advanced counselling is not about mastering a set of "special tricks." It is about presence, creativity, and ethical clarity. The techniques are important, yes, but it is your sincerity, your empathy, and your ability to meet another human being in their suffering that makes the difference.

If you are a lay reader, let these stories remind you that counselling is as much about listening and presence as it is about tools. If you are a professional, may these examples enrich your practice, showing you how CBT, narrative therapy, mindfulness, and solution-focused strategies can merge seamlessly with compassion.

Exercises for Reflection and Practice

1. Reframing Guilt: Think of one situation where you blame yourself. Write down a counter-memory where you acted with care and responsibility. Reflect on how both truths coexist.
2. Pause Before Reacting: In your next stressful interaction, notice your body signals—tightness in jaw, faster breathing. Take three slow breaths before responding. Observe the difference.
3. Finding Purpose in Pain: Recall a loss or setback. Ask yourself: "If the person I lost, or if my future self, could guide me, what would they want me to do now?" Write the answer as a letter to yourself.

These exercises are not substitutes for therapy, but they are practical ways to begin applying advanced counselling principles in everyday life—whether you are helping yourself, guiding a friend, or enriching your professional practice.

As I reflect on my decades of practice, one truth shines brighter than any technique or theory: counselling is sacred work. It is the meeting of two human beings—one in need of healing, the other offering presence, guidance, and respect. Advanced counselling techniques are the tools we carry, but ethics, compassion, and humility are the hands that hold them.

In the words of Viktor Frankl, the Holocaust survivor and psychiatrist who wrote *Man's Search for Meaning* (1946):

"When we are no longer able to change a situation, we are challenged to change ourselves."

This is the essence of advanced counselling: helping people discover that even in the darkest times, they carry within themselves the seeds of light, waiting to grow.

In essence, ethics is the inner compass of counselling. It is what keeps the practice pure, even when methods change. Without ethics, counselling becomes manipulation; with ethics, it becomes healing.

As we will see later in the chapter on legal issues, boundaries and consent also have their procedural dimensions. But ethics is where they begin—not in the law, but in the counsellor's heart.

Key Takeaways

- Advanced counselling is about depth, not complexity. Techniques like narrative therapy, mindfulness, CBT, and solution-focused approaches work best when guided by presence, empathy, and respect.
- Stories shape healing. When clients reframe their narratives—from "I am a failure" to "I am a survivor"—transformation begins.
- The present moment is medicine. Mindfulness allows clients to step out of fear or regret and return to safety in the here and now.

- Integration creates impact. Combining techniques (e.g., CBT for thoughts, mindfulness for grounding, imagery for healing) provides holistic support.
- Ethics is the anchor. Informed consent, clarity about possible risks (like vivid memory-like experiences), and respect for autonomy protect both counsellor and client.
- Cultural sensitivity enriches healing. Spiritual imagery may help one client, scientific explanation another. Both are valid when they honour the client's worldview.
- Transformation is possible. Counselling does not erase pain—it helps people reshape it into strength, purpose, and resilience.

CHAPTER 6

THE HIDDEN DOORWAYS OF HEALING

There are moments in counselling when talk alone does not reach far enough. The client nods, they understand the reasoning, yet something inside remains locked. Words skim the surface of the conscious mind, but the pain, the fear, or the memory sits deeper. For such moments, advanced healing approaches become essential. These are the doorways that lead beyond conversation—into meditation, trance, release, and reconciliation with the inner self.

During the Covid pandemic, these doorways became lifelines. Face-to-face sessions vanished overnight. All counselling had to happen through phone calls—no eye contact, no body language, no reassuring physical presence. Even experienced psychologists, psychiatrists, and medical professionals felt overwhelmed. Many openly admitted, *"We don't know what more to do. Medication alone is not helping."* Some approached me privately and asked, almost in disbelief, *"How are you able to calm patients and guide deep emotional healing using only your voice?"*

Those months tested everything I had learned over five decades. I had to rely entirely on vocal cues—changes in breathing, tremors in speech, prolonged silences—to assess emotional states. Clinically, these are recognised markers of **sympathetic nervous system activation**, associated with acute stress responses such as panic and fear (Thayer & Lane, 2000). By guiding slow diaphragmatic breathing and focused attention, I was consciously facilitating a shift toward **parasympathetic dominance**, promoting calm and physiological regulation—what Stephen Porges describes in his **Polyvagal Theory** as vagal engagement (Porges, 2011).[1]

Yet beyond science, something sacred unfolded. Again and again, I witnessed how human connection—carried only by sound waves across distance—could steady a terrified heart.

One call remains deeply etched in my memory.

A woman rang me and said,

"Sir, I am a doctor. You gave counselling to me and my family when we were all down with Covid, but I never told you that I am a doctor. My brother is now in ICU. He is in extreme panic. His oxygen levels are fluctuating, but more than that, his fear is destroying him. I am sure, if you could speak to him over the phone, he will recover."

She managed to obtain special permission from hospital authorities to briefly bring him out from the ICU area so I could speak to him directly. When I heard his voice, it shook me. He was gasping, convinced death was near. His words came in broken fragments:

"Sir… I can't breathe… I will die… please help me…"

I guided him gently, step by step:

"Slow your breath… in through your nose… out slowly… feel the bed supporting your body… remember your children… their faces… their laughter…"

As he followed my voice, a visible transformation occurred. His respiratory rate slowed. The tremor in his voice reduced. His shoulders relaxed. In clinical terms, his **physiological arousal was decreasing**—a sign of autonomic regulation (Grossman & Taylor, 2007). In spiritual terms, grace was flowing.

By the grace of the Almighty, the change was evident within minutes.

Instead of shifting him back to ICU, the medical team admitted him to a normal ward. From there, his recovery progressed rapidly. Later, his sister called me in tears and said,

"Sir, you didn't just calm him… you gave him the will to live."

This experience humbled me profoundly. It reaffirmed what modern research now confirms—that emotional regulation, positive expectancy, and therapeutic suggestion can influence recovery outcomes through **psychoneuroimmunological pathways** (Ader, 2007).[2] What some call the **placebo response** is now recognised as a genuine mind–body mechanism involving neurotransmitters, immune modulation, and stress hormone regulation (Benedetti, 2014).[3]

It was then I truly understood - presence is not physical. Healing does not depend on a clinic, a couch, or a stethoscope. It depends on how deeply one human being can reach another.

And sometimes, a single voice on a phone becomes a handheld in the dark.

I still remember one of the calls I received during the pandemic

A middle-aged woman, Leela, whispered over the phone, "I know I'm not sick, but I can't breathe. It feels like a hand is pressing my chest." She had tested negative for Covid twice, yet her anxiety convinced her she was dying. Ordinary reassurance wasn't enough. In that moment, I invited her to close her eyes, slow her breathing, and recall the sound of temple bells she had loved as a child. Within minutes, her breath steadied, her shoulders softened, and she said, "For the first time in weeks, I feel safe."

That was therapeutic meditation at work—not mystical, not complex, but profoundly human.

Therapeutic Meditation: A Science of Stillness

Meditation has often been seen as a spiritual practice, but in counselling it becomes a therapeutic tool—a way to calm the nervous system, regulate emotions, and reconnect with inner resources.

Therapeutic meditation differs from traditional meditation in one crucial way: it is guided, intentional, and directed toward healing a psychological issue. Instead of simply "emptying the mind," we focus attention on images, memories, or sensations that restore balance and wellbeing.

Example:

During the pandemic, I guided many anxious patients to remember intensely joyful moments—holding a newborn child, celebrating a graduation, or walking in nature. As they recalled the sights, sounds, and feelings, their bodies began producing the same collective biochemicals—the neurotransmitters, neuropeptides, and hormones—that had originally accompanied those moments. In effect, the body "remembered" happiness, and anxiety dissolved into calm.

As discussed earlier in this book, science supports this. Neuropsychologist Rick Hanson, in *Hardwiring Happiness* (2013), explains how recalling positive experiences rewires the brain toward resilience. Indian psychology has long taught the same principle: when the mind dwells on *sattvic* (pure, uplifting) experiences, the whole being shifts toward balance.

Live Scenario:

One young man, terrified after his father was admitted with Covid, called me in tears: "I can't stop imagining his death." I asked him to close his eyes and recall the day his father taught him to ride a bicycle. As he described the scene—his father's hand on the seat, the laughter when he fell, the triumph of balance—his breath slowed, his voice steadied. By anchoring in that joyful memory, he could face the present crisis with greater strength.

Therapeutic meditation is not escape. It is re-anchoring—showing the body and mind that safety and joy are still available, even in crisis.

Hypnosis and Trance Work Explained Simply

Few words in psychology create as much curiosity and confusion as "hypnosis." Many imagine a magician's trick, a swinging pendulum, or a person losing control. The truth is far simpler—and far more powerful.

Hypnosis, in therapeutic practice, is a state of focused attention and deep relaxation in which the mind becomes more open to positive suggestions. It is not about control; it is about collaboration. The client remains aware, yet the usual chatter of the conscious mind quiets, allowing the subconscious to participate actively in healing.

How It Works in Practice:

Imagine a woman with a long-standing fear of public speaking. In a normal state, her conscious mind floods with self-criticism: "I will forget my words, people will laugh." In trance, the counsellor guides her into relaxation—slowing the breath, focusing on calming imagery. Then, positive suggestions are introduced: "You have spoken clearly before. Your voice is strong. Your audience wants you to succeed." The subconscious absorbs these suggestions without the usual resistance, and over time, her behaviour changes.

Example from My Practice:

During my years abroad, I once worked with a corporate executive who dreaded presentations. In trance, we revisited a memory of him confidently explaining cricket rules to friends as a teenager. We linked that natural confidence to his upcoming board presentation. Later, he reported, "For the first time, I spoke without my heart racing."

Trance is not foreign to us. Each of us enters light trance states daily—when absorbed in a film, lost in music, or daydreaming during a train ride. Therapeutic hypnosis simply uses this natural ability in a structured, healing way.

Even Carl Jung acknowledged the depth of the unconscious, and Milton Erickson, one of the pioneers of modern hypnotherapy, demonstrated how trance could bypass resistance and unlock inner solutions.

Breaking the Myths About Hypnosis

Whenever I introduce hypnosis in counselling, the first reaction I often hear is hesitation. Clients whisper, "Will you control my mind?" or "Will I start doing things I don't want to?" Some even smile nervously and ask if I will make them cluck like a chicken. These fears do not come from reality but from stage shows, films, and exaggerated stories.

The truth is far more reassuring. Hypnosis is not about losing control—it is about gaining it back. In trance, a person is more focused, not less. They are less distracted by the usual noise of the conscious mind, but always aware of their values and surroundings. If I suggested something against their will—such as harming themselves or revealing a secret—they would simply refuse or emerge from trance.

To make it simple, I explain it this way:

"When you are absorbed in a book or a film, you forget time. You know where you are, but your attention is so focused that everything else fades. That is a trance state. Hypnosis simply guides you into that focus deliberately and uses it for healing."

Live Example from Practice

A college student once came to me, terrified of exams. He said, "If you hypnotise me, will I be under your control?" I smiled and replied, "No, you will be more in your own control than ever before. I cannot put an idea inside you—you will only accept what feels right to you." We went ahead with a trance session. Afterward, he laughed and said, "I thought I was supposed to sleep. But I was awake the whole time—just very calm and focused." That is exactly what hypnosis is: calm focus, not unconsciousness.

Common Myths vs. Reality

- Myth: Hypnosis makes you unconscious.

  Reality: You remain awake, aware, and in control.

- Myth: The hypnotist controls your mind.

  Reality: No one can force you to do anything against your morals, values, or beliefs.

- Myth: Only weak-minded people can be hypnotised.

  Reality: In fact, the opposite is true—those with good focus and imagination respond best.

- Myth: Hypnosis is magic or supernatural.

  Reality: Hypnosis is a natural psychological phenomenon, studied scientifically and used clinically across the world.

Indian Roots of Trance and Suggestion

Many people assume that hypnosis is a Western invention. In truth, India has nurtured trance-like practices for thousands of years. The Atharva Veda, one of the four ancient Vedas, contains hymns and rituals designed to calm fear, relieve anxiety, and instil positive states of mind. These practices involved rhythmic chanting, repetition of mantras, and ritual gestures that gently guided the participant into a focused, receptive state.

If you read these verses closely, you will notice how they resemble what modern psychology calls suggestion. For example, a priest would recite verses to a person suffering from fear or pain, repeating affirmations of safety and protection: "You are guarded, you are healed, the gods stand beside you." In that receptive state, the person's mind absorbed the suggestion deeply, and healing followed. This is no different from what we today describe as positive therapeutic suggestion in hypnosis.

Beyond the Vedas, India's long tradition of *dhyana* (meditation) and *japa* (repetition of sacred sounds) also mirrors hypnotic states. Anyone who has repeated a mantra thousands of times knows how the mind becomes still, the body relaxes, and a deeper state of receptivity arises. Modern hypnotherapists use similar principles: rhythm, repetition, focus, and guided imagery.

Even temple rituals carried elements of trance. The steady sound of drums, the scent of incense, and the sight of lamps all created a multisensory environment that stilled the restless mind and made the devotee open to transformation. Far from being foreign, trance is woven into the Indian psyche and spiritual life.

When I explain this to clients, I often say:

"What we call hypnosis today is simply a scientific language for what our ancestors already practised. The Atharva Veda used mantras and rituals; I use words and relaxation techniques. But the purpose is the same: to help the mind enter a healing state."

This perspective not only calms their fear but also instils pride. They no longer see hypnosis as alien or threatening but as a continuation of India's own wisdom—updated for modern science.

Emotional Release and Catharsis: When the Floodgates Open

There are sessions when words stumble and emotions pour out raw. The client tries to speak, but the throat closes, and then come the tears, the sobs, sometimes even trembling or laughter that feels uncontrollable. This is catharsis—the release of emotions that have been locked away for too long.

During the pandemic, one young nurse called me after losing three patients in the same week. At first, she explained her exhaustion, then suddenly fell silent, and the phone filled with the sound of weeping. I said nothing. I let the tears run their course. Ten minutes later, she whispered, "I didn't know I had so much inside me. I feel lighter now."

That is the power of catharsis. For centuries, philosophers have known this truth. Aristotle, in *Poetics*, described how watching Greek tragedies allowed audiences to experience *katharsis*—a cleansing of pity and fear. Modern science confirms it: research by Dr. William Frey at the University of Minnesota found that emotional tears contain stress-related chemicals like cortisol. Crying literally detoxifies the body.

But catharsis isn't always tears. Sometimes it is sudden laughter after recounting a painful memory. Sometimes it is anger expressed in safe ways, such as speaking fiercely into a cushion or pounding fists into a pillow. The release itself does not "solve" the problem, but it opens the door for clarity and healing. The counsellor's role is not to restrain it but to hold it safely, ensuring that the client returns to balance afterward.

Trauma Healing: Reclaiming Life from Fear

Trauma is different from ordinary distress. It is not just something remembered; it is something relived. The body behaves as if the past event is happening again in the present. A car horn, a crowded room, even a smell can pull a person back into the fire of memory.

Case Example – The Chartered Accountant from Kolkata

One of my most challenging but rewarding cases involved a brilliant chartered accountant. Outwardly, she was successful, managing complex accounts for multinational clients. Inwardly, she was imprisoned. She could not board a flight, paralysed by the thought of being trapped in the air. Train journeys were equally impossible because of her phobia of using public toilets. Severe allergies weakened her further, and her marriage was on the verge of collapse. She told me, "I can balance anyone's books, but not my own life."

We began with guided imagery exposure. In a relaxed state, I asked her to imagine walking into an airport. At first, even the image of the boarding gate made her palms sweat. We paused, anchored her in deep breathing, and I reminded her, "You are safe here in this room." The next session, she visualised sitting in an airplane seat, fastening the belt, hearing the hum of engines. Each step was small, but each victory trained her subconscious that safety was possible. Months later, she boarded a short flight for the first time in years.

Her fear of train toilets was addressed with systematic desensitisation. In trance, she pictured herself entering a clean restroom, then gradually imagined less comfortable ones, each time practising calm breathing. Slowly, the subconscious fear dissolved.

But her greatest struggle was with her marriage. Her husband had grown distant, calling her "fragile" and "difficult." In trance dialogue, we explored her belief: "I am a burden." This belief drove both her phobias and her marital pain. I asked her to recall times of strength—academic awards, challenging cases solved, difficult clients managed. Her body straightened as she recounted them. Slowly, she reframed her identity: not "a burden," but "a fighter who overcomes." With counselling, her relationship began to heal, and she rediscovered self-respect.

This case taught me that trauma is not confined to one symptom—it spreads into travel, health, career, and love. Healing is not about removing a fear; it is about giving life back its wholeness.

Inner Conflicts: The Battles of the Mind

Not all pain comes from external events. Some of the deepest struggles are inner conflicts—when two parts of the self pull in opposite directions.

Case Example – The Executive and the Writer Within

Meera, a corporate executive, came to me exhausted. Her body was fine, her career successful, yet she felt "tired for no reason." When we explored further, she confessed, "I want to be a writer. But if I leave my job, I'll disappoint everyone who believes in me." Her subconscious was at war: security versus passion.

To externalise this, I used the empty chair dialogue. I placed two chairs before her: one for the corporate self, one for the creative self. She sat in the corporate chair and said sternly: "I give you stability. I pay the bills. I earned the respect of society. Without me, you'd be nothing." Then she moved to the creative chair, her eyes softening: "You may give me money, but I give you soul. Without me, you're a machine."

Back and forth the dialogue raged—accusations, defences, pleas. Then something shifted. She began to notice her body in each chair: tight jaw and shallow breath as the corporate self, open chest and laughter as the creative self. By becoming aware of these subconscious cues, she discovered that neither side was the enemy. She did not need to kill one self to honour the other. The solution came naturally: she kept her job for stability but began writing short stories on weekends. Her fatigue lifted because her selves were no longer at war.

Indian Philosophy: The Battlefield Within

Indian philosophy has long understood trauma and conflict. The Upanishads describe the mind as layered, storing impressions (*samskaras*) that shape our present reactions. Trauma is one such *samskara*—replaying until it is recognised and integrated. Healing means not suppressing it but transforming it.

The Bhagavad Gita offers perhaps the greatest example of counselling in the face of inner conflict. Arjuna, paralysed on the battlefield, says,

"My limbs give way, my mouth is dry, my body trembles, my hair stands on end."

(Bhagavad Gita 1:29, translated by Swami Prabhavananda & Christopher Isherwood, 1944)

This is trauma in poetic form. Krishna does not scold him; he listens, then patiently guides him. He reframes duty (*dharma*), reveals perspective, and helps Arjuna integrate fear with action.

When I work with clients paralysed by inner conflict, I often say,

"You are like Arjuna—your chariot has stopped. My role is not to fight your battle but to help you hear your own Krishna—the wisdom inside you that knows the way."

Integration: Healing Beyond Words

Catharsis empties the burden. Trauma healing reclaims safety. Empty chair dialogue restores inner peace. Indian wisdom reframes conflict as *dharma*. Together, they show that advanced healing approaches are not mechanical tricks—they are sacred dialogues between counsellor and client, between conscious and subconscious, between the wounded self and the wiser self.

Integration: A Symphony of Healing

If basic counselling is like learning the grammar of human connection, advanced healing approaches are like poetry. They move beyond the surface of words into the rhythms of the subconscious and the body's silent memory.

Meditation teaches the body to remember calm.

Hypnosis helps the subconscious cooperate with healing instead of resisting it.

Catharsis clears the heaviness of unexpressed emotion.

Trauma work restores safety where the body still trembles.

Conflict resolution reconciles the battles within.

Together, these are not separate tools but a symphony—different instruments playing toward one harmony: the healing of the person. And as with any music, the counsellor's role is not to dominate but to conduct gently, ensuring balance, timing, and flow.

I have seen executives rediscover focus, young mothers release guilt, students overcome exam panic, couples rebuild intimacy, and trauma survivors walk free from memories that once imprisoned them. Each of these victories was not the result of one method alone, but of attentive presence combined with the right technique at the right time.

As the Brihadaranyaka Upanishad reminds us,

"As is your deepest desire, so is your will; as is your will, so is your deed; as is your deed, so is your destiny."

Advanced healing approaches simply help clients reshape their deepest desires and inner states so that their actions and destinies change accordingly.

Practical Exercises for Readers

While many advanced techniques require training, there are safe practices every reader can begin today. These simple exercises reflect the spirit of therapeutic meditation, guided imagery, and catharsis:

1. **Memory Anchor Exercise**
   - Sit comfortably and recall a vivid, joyful memory (a family celebration, a quiet morning in nature).
   - Close your eyes, breathe slowly, and relive it with all senses—what you saw, heard, smelled, and felt.
   - As you immerse yourself, lightly press your thumb and forefinger together. Repeat a phrase like "Safe now" or "Peace is here."
   - Practise daily. Soon, pressing your fingers together will trigger calm even in stressful situations.

2. **Safe Place Visualization**
   - Imagine a place where you feel completely secure (a beach, a temple, a mountain path).
   - Spend five minutes exploring this place in detail—colours, sounds, textures.
   - Use this "safe place" before sleep or after recalling a difficult memory.

3. **Cathartic Writing**
   - Write freely about a strong emotion.
   - Write until you feel a shift.
   - Tear or discard the paper safely.

4. **Inner Dialogue Practice**
   - Write a dialogue between your critic and defender.
   - Then write as a mediator finding balance.

Key Takeaways

- Therapeutic meditation anchors safety.
- Hypnosis is natural and rooted in Indian traditions.
- Catharsis clears suppressed emotions.
- Trauma work restores safety.
- Inner conflict resolution harmonises the self.
- Indian philosophy echoes modern counselling.
- Healing is presence, timing, and guidance.

Closing Reflection

Advanced healing approaches are sacred bridges. They connect the conscious and subconscious, the present and the past, the fragmented self and the whole. Whether through meditation, trance, tears, or dialogue, each step reminds us that healing is not imposed from outside—it awakens from within.

As counsellors, psychologists, doctors, or simply as human beings, we must remember:

We are not fixing people.

We are companions helping them rediscover what was never lost—their own strength, wisdom, and capacity for joy.

CHAPTER 7

THE COUNSELLING JOURNEY: FROM FIRST CONTACT TO CLOSURE

A Whisper That Begins a Journey

Counselling rarely begins with a dramatic breakdown or a loud cry for help. More often, it begins with a whisper. A hesitant message typed and deleted twice before being sent. A short email written late at night. A phone call made with trembling fingers. The voice on the other end is cautious, almost apologetic, as if the person feels guilty for needing help.

"Sir, can I talk? I don't know what's wrong with me, but I can't go on like this."

Behind these simple words lies immense courage. Reaching out means admitting vulnerability in a world that celebrates strength. It means standing at the edge of the unknown, not knowing whether one will be judged, misunderstood, or truly heard. Many people suffer silently for years before sending that first message. That whisper itself is a victory over fear.

I remember one such call during the height of the Covid pandemic. It was past midnight. The house was quiet. My phone lit up with a message from Harish, a 32-year-old sales manager.

"Sir, I can't sleep. My heart races all night. I feel like something terrible will happen."

His words felt rushed, breathless, almost panicked. There was an urgency in them, but also hesitation—as if he was afraid of disturbing me, afraid of being a burden. Yet what he had done was remarkable. He had reached out. He had chosen connection over isolation.

When I called him back, he spoke quickly, as if words might escape him if he paused. He described a tightness in his chest, nights spent staring at the ceiling, thoughts racing in circles, fear rising without reason, exhaustion that sleep never cured.

"I feel like I'm running all the time, sir… even in bed," he said.

Instead of jumping into advice or diagnosis, I slowed the pace.

"Harish," I said gently, "you've done the right thing by reaching out. You're not alone in this. We'll work through it together."

There was silence. A long pause. Then I heard him exhale deeply, as if he had been holding his breath for days.

"Thank you," he whispered. "I already feel better."

Nothing in his outer world had changed. His job was the same. His problems were still there. But something profound had happened—he felt heard.

That moment reminded me of a truth I have seen repeatedly over decades:

Healing often begins not with solutions, but with presence.

Not with techniques, but with connection.

Not with answers, but with being understood.

Long before counselling methods, assessments, or strategies come into play, the simple act of being listened to plants the first seed of recovery. The whisper becomes a doorway.

The Intake: Listening for Threads, Not Labels

When Harish came for his first in-person session, he did not sit back in the chair. He perched on its edge—as if unsure whether he was allowed to settle.

His shoulders were raised slightly.
His fingers were tightly interlocked.
His feet angled toward the door.

His body had arrived before his trust did.

Before he spoke a single word, his posture told me something important: this was a man who had been bracing for a long time.

Many imagine intake as a structured checklist:

Name.
Age.
Occupation.
Symptoms.
Duration.

And yes—these details matter.

But true intake is not the completion of a form.
It is the beginning of a relationship.
It is not data collection.
It is pattern recognition.

You do not merely gather facts—you listen for threads. Emotional threads. Physiological threads. Historical threads. You listen for what is spoken easily, what is rehearsed, what trembles, and what is carefully avoided.

I asked Harish about his sleep.
He answered precisely.
About his appetite.
Measured response.
About his work routine.
Clear, structured, controlled.

He spoke like a man presenting a performance report.

But while he spoke, his body revealed more.

When he mentioned his boss, his jaw tightened almost imperceptibly.
When he described deadlines, his shoulders sagged—as though carrying invisible weight.
But when he spoke about his mother rising before dawn to pray, something shifted.
His breath slowed.
His tone softened.
His face relaxed.

There—in that subtle physiological change—was safety.

The conscious story he presented was insomnia.

The deeper story, however, lived elsewhere—in chronic pressure, in fear of failure, in the quiet exhaustion of never feeling enough. His emotional–biochemical system had been running on sustained alert. Cortisol had become his companion. Rest had begun to feel unfamiliar—even unsafe.

This is where many professionals rush forward.

"Anxiety disorder."
"Occupational stress."
"Adjustment difficulty."

Labels can describe.

But they do not yet understand.

And understanding must precede intervention.

Intake is where the counsellor must deliberately slow down—not to delay help, but to deepen it. A diagnosis may clarify a cluster of symptoms, but it does not illuminate the inner landscape of the person sitting before you.

Instead of categorising him, I reflected what I sensed:

"It sounds like your body is running a race long after the day has ended. Your mind may have learnt that slowing down is risky—that vigilance equals safety. Shall we gently explore whether it is possible to teach your system a different rhythm?"

He looked up then.

Not with resistance.
Not with defensiveness.

But with relief.

"Yes… that's exactly it," he said quietly.

For the first time, he did not feel examined.

He did not feel reduced to a condition.

He felt seen.

And in that moment, something subtle happened. His breathing deepened. His shoulders lowered slightly. The room shifted from evaluation to safety.

That shift—that physiological settling—is often the first real sign that trust has begun.

And trust is the foundation of all healing.

Another experience during the Covid crisis reaffirmed this truth with even greater intensity.

A young medical intern once told me over the phone:

"I'm fine during the day, sir. I can function. I can treat patients. But at night… I hear the cries of those I lost."

Her intake was not about medical history.

It was about grief.

Survivor's guilt.

Unprocessed sorrow stored in the nervous system.

She did not need advice about resilience.
She did not need motivational language.

She needed permission to mourn.

As she spoke, her voice broke. Tears followed. I did not interrupt. I did not rush to reassure. I did not attempt to neutralise the pain with logic.

I simply stayed.

Silence, in that moment, was not absence. It was containment.

Her sobbing gradually softened. Her breath, initially uneven, steadied. After a long pause, she said:

"Thank you for not stopping me."

Those words have remained with me.

Because in that moment, intake was not assessment.

It was acknowledgement.

Listening itself became therapy.

Over five decades, I have learned this repeatedly:

Intake is not about discovering what is wrong.

It is about discovering what hurts.

It is about sensing where the emotional–biochemical system has been strained, where vigilance has replaced rest, where grief has been postponed, where identity has narrowed under pressure.

When a person feels safe enough to reveal that hidden place,

the journey of healing has already begun.

Not because solutions have been given—

but because understanding has taken root.

Formulation: A Map the Client Can Read

Once intake begins to reveal the emotional threads of a person's life, formulation is about weaving those threads into something coherent.

Not a secret clinical document tucked away in the counsellor's file.

But a living map.

A map the client can see.
Understand.
Question.
And eventually walk through with confidence.

I often tell clients,

"If you don't understand your own map, how will you know where you are going?"

Formulation is not diagnosis in complicated language. It is translation. It takes scattered experiences—symptoms, memories, triggers, habits—and arranges them into a pattern that makes sense. When confusion becomes structure, fear begins to loosen.

With Harish, we did not create this map in one dramatic session. It emerged gently, over time, as trust deepened and honesty became easier.

His map slowly revealed:

A demanding sales role with unpredictable targets
A harsh inner critic shaped by early academic scrutiny
A new supervisor whose tone unconsciously echoed old authority figures
Night-time habits—coffee, endless phone scrolling, late news exposure
A nervous system chronically locked in "emergency mode"

None of these alone explained his insomnia.

Together, they did.

I explained it to him in simple language:

"Harish, imagine you trained your mind to be a security guard who never sleeps. Even when there is no real danger, he keeps shouting, 'Alert! Alert!' Your body listens. Your heart races. Sleep disappears. Muscles stay tense. This is not weakness. It is conditioning."

He sat very still.

"So I am not weak?" he asked, almost hesitantly.

"No," I smiled gently. "Your system is overprotective. It learnt vigilance somewhere in life. It was trying to help you. Now we will teach it a new lesson."

In that moment, something shifted inside him.

His suffering was no longer mysterious.

It had structure.

And what has structure can be reshaped.

When people understand that their reactions are patterned—not random—the shame reduces. The emotional–biochemical storm begins to feel less like a personal flaw and more like a predictable cascade. And what is predictable can be interrupted.

I witnessed the same transformation during telephonic Covid counselling.

One caller gasped over the phone:

"Sir… I think I will die tonight."

His breathing was rapid. Words came in fragments. Panic had already taken hold.

Instead of dismissing his fear with reassurance, I began gently mapping the sequence.

"What made the fear start tonight?"
"Did something happen before the panic began?"

Slowly, the story unfolded.

Ambulance sirens in the street.
Hours of scrolling through death statistics.
A neighbour who had passed away that morning.

We drew the pattern together:

External trigger →
Catastrophic thought ("I am next") →
Body panic (breathless, shaking, chest tight) →
More catastrophic thought →
More panic

There was a long pause on the line.

Then he said softly,

"So… I am not dying. I am reacting to fear."

That insight was medicine.

The moment the map became visible, the panic lost some of its authority. His breath began to lengthen. His voice steadied. The spiral loosened.

Formulation gave him clarity.

Clarity gave him distance.

Distance gave him control.

Over decades, I have learned something simple and humbling:

People are rarely broken.

They are often misinformed about their own patterns.

They believe the reaction is the reality.

Formulation gently reveals:

"This is not who you are. This is how your system has been trained."

And when a person can see their own map clearly,

they stop feeling lost.

They begin to navigate.

From Vague Hopes to Living Goals

Most clients arrive with beautiful but vague wishes.

"I just want peace."

"I want to feel normal."

"I want to stop thinking."

These are heartfelt—but the mind cannot walk toward a cloud.

It needs direction.

So we transform wishes into living goals—goals the body and subconscious can understand.

With Harish, we made his goals concrete:

- Fall asleep within 20 minutes
- Reduce awakenings from three to one
- Enter Monday meetings without panic
- Switch off the phone by 10:30 p.m.

When he saw them written, he smiled.

"This feels possible," he said.

That is the magic of clear goals.

They give hope *structure.*

Another case touched me deeply. A widow who lost her husband during Covid told me:

"I want him back."

Her pain was raw.

Of course she wanted him back.

But slowly, gently, we reshaped the goal.

After many tears, she said:

"I want to remember him with love… not only pain.

I want to continue our morning walks… for him."

Now she had a path forward.

Grief had direction.

Memory became honour.

I told her:

"You cannot change the past.

But you can change how you carry it."

Goals are not about control.

They are about meaning.

In counselling, this step is sacred.

We move from:

"I don't want this pain"

to

"This is how I want to live."

That shift alone transforms people.

The Middle Sessions: The Classroom of Change

Middle sessions are where real change is rehearsed. If the first sessions are about understanding and insight, the middle phase is about *practice*. This is the classroom where the client learns new emotional habits, stumbles, corrects, and slowly strengthens.

With Harish, change did not happen in dramatic leaps. It happened in small, almost invisible steps.

We began with breathing. At first, he was impatient.

"How will breathing change my life, sir?" he asked with a half-smile.

I told him,

"Because your breath is the remote control of your nervous system."

He practised slow inhalation and longer exhalation. To make it personal, I asked him to anchor the breath to a comforting memory. He chose mornings with his mother—tea on the balcony, temple bells in the distance, birds starting their day.

As he breathed, I asked him to gently press his thumb and forefinger together and whisper,

"Safe now."

That small gesture became powerful.

A portable anchor.

A silent signal to his body.

Weeks later he said,

"Sir, last night I woke up at 3 a.m. Normally I panic. This time I pressed my fingers and said 'Safe now.' I slept again."

For him, this was a victory.

We also worked on thoughts that attacked him at night.

"If I don't sleep, tomorrow is ruined."

"If I make one mistake, my boss will fire me."

We rewrote them together:

"Sleep matters, but one bad night won't destroy my life."

"Mistakes are human. One meeting does not define me."

Sometimes humour worked better than logic.

One Monday he laughed,

"The meeting was still a circus, sir... but I didn't join every act!"

That laughter was healing.

It meant distance from fear.

For a student with exam panic, we practised grounding.

Whenever her heart raced, she named:

- 5 things she could see
- 4 things she could touch
- 3 sounds she could hear

This pulled her out of panic and into the present.

Slowly, week by week, I saw something change in their eyes.

Less fear.

More confidence.

Middle sessions teach an important truth:

Change is not dramatic.

It is disciplined.

Gentle.

Repeated.

Ruptures and Repairs: The Hidden Strength

Not every session is smooth. There are days when clients resist, forget homework, arrive late, or even get angry.

These moments are called *ruptures*.

But here is a secret most people don't know:

Ruptures, when repaired, deepen trust.

One day Harish snapped,

"Breathing won't change my boss, sir!"

I smiled and said,

"You're right.

Breathing won't change him.

But it might change who shows up to meet him."

He stared at me, then laughed.

"You're dangerous," he joked.

That moment shifted something.

We were equals now.

Not therapist and patient—two humans.

During Covid tele-counselling, a patient once said angrily,

"You don't know what this feels like!"

I didn't defend myself.

I didn't argue.

I said honestly,

"You are right.

I don't know *your* exact pain.

But I know fear.

And I know the human mind.

Let's face it together."

There was silence.

Then he said,

"Thank you for not pretending."

That honesty healed the rupture.

Ruptures teach clients something precious:

Relationships don't have to break when conflict appears.

They can bend.

Repair.

Grow.

Many clients carry this lesson into marriages, offices, and friendships.

Handling Crises: When the Storm Hits

Progress in counselling does not mean storms will never return. Life does not wait for therapy to finish. Losses happen. Jobs change. Bodies fall sick. Relationships break. When such moments strike, the counsellor becomes both harbour and lighthouse—offering shelter while pointing toward safety.

With Harish, the storm came unexpectedly.

One afternoon he messaged:

"Sir, my company announced layoffs."

His old fears rushed back. That familiar tightness returned to his chest. The night before our session, he hardly slept.

Instead of false reassurance, I told him,

"Fear is natural. Let us prepare rather than panic."

Together, we created a *crisis plan*:

- Whom he would call when anxiety spiked
- Which breathing ritual he would repeat
- What grounding statement he would use
- How he would limit news exposure

I asked him to write it down and keep it near his bed.

The next week he said,

"Sir, I followed the plan.

I was scared… but I didn't collapse."

That is courage.

In more severe crises—suicidal thoughts, hallucinations, extreme withdrawal—the responsibility of a counsellor is clear:

Referral is not retreat.

It is professionalism.

Sending someone for psychiatric support is not failure.

It is protecting life.

I tell my students:

"When you refer, you are not stepping back.

You are stepping up."

Family Involvement: Allies, Not Judges

Counselling rarely happens in isolation.

Behind every client stands a family—sometimes supportive, sometimes unknowingly harmful.

With Harish, his wife joined one session. She looked worried but hopeful.

I asked her,

"What do you notice on days he sleeps well?"

She thought and said,

"He leaves his phone outside the bedroom."

That became a family ritual.

She also learnt to place her hand gently on his shoulder at night and whisper,

"Breathe with me."

That small act changed everything.

From:

"Why can't you sleep?"

to

"We will breathe together."

Their marriage shifted from tension to teamwork.

With a teenage girl facing exam anxiety, her parents unknowingly increased pressure.

"She must score high."

"Competition is tough."

I reframed gently:

"She does not need pressure.

She needs your faith."

They softened.

Praise replaced criticism.

Encouragement replaced threats.

Her grades improved—not because of fear, but confidence.

Family involvement works best when:

- Guided respectfully
- With client consent
- Framed as support, not judgment

Families, when aligned, become healing teams.

Ending as a Skill, Not an Accident

Closure is not something that "just happens."

It is not an abrupt goodbye.

It is a skill—a deliberate act of healing.

With Harish, we did not simply stop sessions one day and move on. We prepared for closure the same way we prepared for change.

We reviewed his journey:

- How his sleep had improved
- How his panic had reduced
- How he now faced meetings with steadiness

Then I asked him,

"What tools do you now carry?"

He smiled and listed them:

"Breathing… the finger anchor… limiting my phone… reframing thoughts… calling my wife instead of scrolling."

That awareness was powerful.

Then I gave him a final task.

I asked him to write a letter.

Not to me.

To himself.

A letter from his *steady self* to his *3 a.m. self.*

When he read it aloud, his voice trembled:

"Dear Harish,

You are safe.

You have survived worse days.

One bad night does not define your life.

Breathe.

Morning will come."

Silence filled the room.

"That letter," he said,

"I will keep it near my bed."

We also planned follow-ups—one month, three months.

Not to control him.

But to ensure he never felt abandoned.

Closure is not a slammed door.

It is a gentle release.

Like a teacher watching a student walk out of class for the last time—proud, hopeful, trusting.

Another case was Sana, a 19-year-old who compulsively fought online debates. Every disagreement felt personal to her. She needed to win to feel worthy.

For closure, she created a ritual.

She bought a notebook and wrote on the first page:

"Enough for Today."

Every time she wanted to argue, she wrote instead.

In her final session, she smiled shyly:

"Sir, I still like debates…

but I don't need to be the judge anymore."

That is growth.

Each journey has its own music.

But the arc remains the same:

From chaos → to clarity

From compulsion → to choice

Indian Wisdom: The Journey as a *Yatra*

In Indian tradition, a *yatra* (pilgrimage) begins with uncertainty. The traveller leaves the comfort of home, walks through fatigue, doubt, and discovery, and finally reaches the sanctum—not to receive something new, but to realise what was always within.

Counselling mirrors this journey.

The client begins at the outer gate of distress.

Fear in the heart.

Questions in the mind.

The techniques—reframing, meditation, dialogue—are like rituals along the path.

Closure is the sanctum.

The discovery:

"I was always capable."

"I was never broken."

"Healing lived inside me."

The Bhagavad Gita captures this truth beautifully.

Arjuna trembles on the battlefield:

"My limbs give way, my mouth is dry, my body trembles."

Krishna does not fight for him.

He guides him.

In the same way, the counsellor is not the warrior.

The counsellor is the guide.

Helping the client find their own *dharma*.

Their own wisdom.

Their own strength.

Over five decades of practice, I have learned something simple yet profound:

Counselling is not about dramatic breakthroughs.

It is about faithful journeys.

The first contact plants hope.

Intake gathers the threads.

Formulation offers a map.

Goals give direction.

Middle sessions rehearse change.

Ruptures test trust.

Crises demand steady hands.

Families become allies.

Closure releases the client into their own strength.

As counsellors:

We are gardeners, watering growth patiently.

We are conductors, ensuring harmony.

Above all, we are companions—

Present when another human being whispers,

"Please help."

And willing to walk beside them

until they can walk alone.

Key Takeaways

- The first contact itself is therapeutic—listening plants hope.
- Intake means listening for emotional threads, not just data.
- Formulation offers a shared map the client can understand.
- Goals transform vague wishes into living direction.

- Middle sessions rehearse new habits with patience and practice.
- Ruptures, when repaired, deepen trust and safety.
- Crises require preparation and sometimes referral.
- Families become allies when guided with respect.
- Closure is a skill—ending with dignity and ritual.
- Counselling mirrors a pilgrimage (*yatra*): from distress to discovery.

Practical Exercises

1. First Contact Rehearsal
2. Imagine a friend says, "I can't go on."
3. Practise responding with reassurance, not advice.
4. Formulation Sketch
5. Write your own:
6. Trigger → Thought → Emotion → Behaviour chain.
7. Goal Shaping
8. Replace one vague wish with a measurable action.
9. Rupture Repair Drill
10. Recall a conflict.
11. Write how you could repair trust.
12. Closure Ritual
13. Write a letter from your "steady self" to your "distressed self."
14. Keep it for difficult times.

Reflective Questions

- When did I last truly listen without interrupting?
- What patterns repeat in my emotional reactions?
- How do I respond to crises—avoid or prepare?
- Who in my family could be an ally?
- What would closure look like in my life right now?

CHAPTER 8

OVERCOMING RESISTANCE

When the Door Is Half-Closed

Counselling is not always a smooth path where the client pours out their soul and the counsellor guides them gently towards healing. Often, the very first encounter feels like standing before a half-closed door. You knock, you wait, you invite—but the door does not swing open easily.

Anjali was one such client. Her parents brought her to me, anxious and insistent:

"She doesn't talk to us anymore.-Please, make her normal again."

Anjali sat down, her body folded inwards, her eyes fixed on the floor. I asked gently,

"What brings you here today?"

She shrugged. Another question, another shrug. Finally, she said, her voice sharp with hopelessness:

"Talking won't help. Nothing helps."

To many people, this looks like defiance. To me, it was protection. Her silence was not laziness; it was armour. Somewhere in her life, she had been hurt, dismissed, or judged. Now she was saying without words:

"I cannot risk being vulnerable again. If I don't speak, I cannot be wounded."

I did not push her. Instead, I leaned back and said softly:

"That's alright, Anjali. We don't have to talk today. Silence is also part of the story."

For the first time, her eyes lifted from the floor to meet mine. That small glance was not a breakthrough, but it was a crack in the wall.

This is the paradox of resistance. It feels like an obstacle, but in truth it is the subconscious whispering:

"I am not ready yet. Go slowly."

The counsellor's role is not to smash the door open, but to stand patiently outside until the client feels safe enough to open it themselves.

Why Clients Resist Change

At first glance, resistance seems irrational. Why would anyone resist freedom from pain?

But if you listen closely, resistance always follows a logic.

Harish, the sales manager I worked with, once said during a session:

"I know my insomnia is killing me. But at least I know how to live with it. I don't know who I'd be without it."

He hated his sleepless nights, yet he clung to them. Why? Because insomnia, though painful, was familiar. The unknown—life without it—felt riskier.

A corporate leader explained his aggression in similar terms:

"If I stop shouting, my team will walk all over me."

His aggression was destroying trust, but to him it felt like armour. Letting it go was not liberation—it felt like walking naked into battle.

And then there are the hidden benefits, the "secondary gains."

One young woman confessed:

"When I am anxious, my parents never leave me alone. If I get better, will they still care for me this much?"

For her, anxiety was also a guarantee of attention.

Resistance also comes from the subconscious itself. The mind buries painful memories the way the body grows a scab. Peel it too soon, and the wound bleeds. The subconscious resists not to frustrate the counsellor, but to protect the person from overwhelm.

The Bhagavad Gita offers perhaps the most timeless portrait of resistance.

On the battlefield of Kurukshetra, Arjuna lays down his bow, trembling:

"My limbs give way, my mouth is dry, my body trembles, my hair stands on end… I will not fight."

(Bhagavad Gita, 1:29–30)

This is resistance in its purest form: the paralysis of fear, the refusal to move forward even when duty is clear. Krishna does not shame him; he listens, then patiently guides him through the fog. Every counsellor has met an Arjuna in their practice.

Denial: The First Wall

Denial is perhaps the most familiar face of resistance. It arrives with a smile and a shake of the head:

"I don't have a problem. Others are exaggerating."

A corporate executive, referred to me for drinking issues, greeted me warmly:

"They think I drink too much. Honestly, it's just one or two in the evening. I can stop anytime."

I didn't confront him. Instead, I asked:

"Tell me about those evenings. Walk me through them."

He started describing—one drink before dinner, another with the meal, a third after dessert, then perhaps a nightcap. By the time he finished, his "one or two" had quietly multiplied into five. He stopped mid-sentence, frowned, and gave me a sheepish smile:

"Well… maybe I underestimated."

That was the first crack in the wall. Not because I accused him, but because I let him hear his own truth.

Denial is not always a deliberate lie.

It is often the mind's way of saying:

"I cannot face the whole truth yet. Let me take it in small doses."

A wise counsellor respects that pacing.

Another case:

During my COVID counselling calls, I often heard denial in different forms. A breathless patient would insist,

"It's just a little cold. Nothing serious."

Even when oxygen levels were dropping, they clung to denial.

Why? Because to admit the truth was to face death. Resistance here was not foolishness—it was survival.

Projection: The Mirror Turned Outward

Projection is resistance wearing another mask.

Instead of saying "I am afraid," the client says,

"They are out to get me."

One night during the pandemic, a man called me in fury:

"The government is trying to kill us. Doctors don't care. My neighbours want me to collapse."

His voice was sharp, but beneath it trembled fear.

I didn't debate his accusations. Instead, I asked softly:

"What does it feel like in your body right now, when you say this?"

There was silence. Then his voice cracked:

"It feels like my chest is locked. Like I can't breathe."

That was the moment the mirror turned inward.

He realised his fear was not only "out there"—it was inside him.

Once the blame dissolved, the real work of healing could begin.

Projection is the subconscious saying:

"This emotion is too heavy for me. Let me hang it on someone else's shoulders."

The counsellor's task is to gently turn the mirror back, until the client recognises their own reflection—not with shame, but with compassion.

Transference: Old Shadows in New Rooms

Sometimes resistance doesn't appear as silence or denial. Sometimes it enters the room disguised as an old ghost. A client looks at you, the counsellor, but sees someone else entirely—a father, a teacher, a partner. This is transference.

I once counselled a young man named Ramesh. He had a tense relationship with his strict father, who always judged him harshly. In our sessions, whenever I asked a clarifying question, Ramesh's voice grew defensive:

"Why are you criticising me? Why do you always assume I'm wrong?"

In truth, I wasn't criticising at all. But in his eyes, I had become his father. The counselling room had turned into his childhood dining table.

Instead of denying it, I leaned into the moment:

"Ramesh, I notice that when I ask you questions, you hear criticism. Could it be that I remind you of someone who used to criticise you?"

He froze, then whispered:

"You sound like my father."

Tears welled in his eyes. That recognition was powerful. It shifted the energy of our sessions. He realised that he was not arguing with me, but with the ghost of his father.

By naming the transference, we turned resistance into a doorway for healing.

Another case example:

During my COVID telephonic counselling, a woman told me,

"You therapists are all the same. You only care because you're paid. Just like doctors who ignore patients once they get their money."

At first, I felt hurt—but then I realised: she wasn't talking to me. She was reliving past disappointment with healthcare providers.

I said gently:

"It sounds like you've felt abandoned before. Maybe by doctors or others you trusted. Is that true?"

She broke down crying.

"Yes. When my husband was sick, no one cared."

Her anger at me was really her unprocessed grief. Once we named it, the wall softened, and she was able to engage with me more openly.

This is the paradox of transference: it resists counselling by replaying old relationships, but if addressed with care, it opens a deeper level of healing than anything else.

Techniques to Soften Resistance: Walking Beside the Wall

Over decades of practice, I have learnt that resistance is not broken by force. It is softened, like clay in warm water. And the tools to soften it are not complicated—they are rooted in respect, patience, and creativity.

1. The Power of Metaphor

Sometimes a direct challenge only strengthens resistance. But metaphor can bypass the conscious defences.

I once told a hesitant client:

"Imagine your life as a house. Some rooms you keep tidy and open. But there's a locked storeroom. You avoid it because it feels dusty and dark. My role isn't to break the lock. It's to hold the lamp while you decide when to enter."

The client nodded silently. Later she said,

"For the first time, I felt you weren't pushing me—you were waiting with me."

The metaphor spoke to her subconscious in a way plain logic could not.

2. Pacing the Client's Rhythm

A counsellor once told me in training:

"Never run faster than the client can walk."

Resistance often eases when you respect the client's pace.

During my work with a phobic chartered accountant from Kolkata, I didn't force her onto a plane on day one. We started with imagining the airport lounge. Then the boarding gate. Then fastening the belt. Each step respected her rhythm.

The slowness was not delay—it was healing in motion.

3. Reframing Resistance Itself

Sometimes the best way to soften resistance is to redefine it.

An executive once told me, arms crossed:

"I'm not going to waste time on breathing exercises. I'm too practical for this nonsense."

Instead of arguing, I reframed:

"Then let's call it a focus drill. You're not breathing to relax—you're training your body like an athlete prepares before a match."

His eyes lit up. He practised eagerly.

The same technique, repackaged, bypassed resistance.

4. Humour as a Gentle Lever

There are moments when laughter achieves what logic cannot.

Harish, in one of his sleepless nights, snapped:

"This is useless. Breathing won't change my boss!"

I replied, smiling:

"True. But at least it will change the man who has to listen to your boss."

He laughed. The wall cracked.

Humour had softened the resistance without diminishing the seriousness of his struggle.

A Case of Layers: Resistance as Teacher

One of my most memorable cases was during the pandemic. A middle-aged man called me, his voice heavy with frustration:

"Don't start your therapist talk. I don't need counselling. I just need this fear to go away."

I could have argued. Instead, I asked,

"Then why did you call me tonight?"

He paused.

"Because I can't breathe properly, and I don't want to scare my wife."

That was the real story. His resistance wasn't against counselling. It was against appearing weak in front of his family.

Once he admitted that, the wall softened. He said, almost shyly:

"Maybe… talking does help."

This man taught me something I never forgot: resistance is not just a barrier. It is also a teacher. It shows us where the client feels most vulnerable, most protective, most afraid. If we learn to listen to resistance, it guides us straight to the wound that needs healing.

Case-Based Deep Dives: Resistance in Action

Resistance does not wear one face. It changes depending on the person, the context, and the hidden wound. Let me take you through a few more cases that reveal its many colours.

The Teenager in Denial

Ritika, a 16-year-old, was failing her exams. Her parents brought her to me, worried she was spending all her time on her phone. Ritika rolled her eyes and said,

"They're exaggerating. Everyone studies less in 11th grade. I'm fine."

Her denial was thick. I didn't confront her. Instead, I asked,

"What do you enjoy most on your phone?"

She lit up, talking about dance videos and friends. As she relaxed, I gently asked,

"And when exams come close, how do you manage then?"

Her voice dropped:

"I panic. I can't focus."

The wall of denial cracked. She admitted she needed help—not because I forced her, but because I first honoured her joy. Denial faded once she felt safe enough to tell the truth.

The Executive Who Projected His Anxiety

A corporate supervisor stormed into my office:

"My team is useless. Lazy. They don't respect me. That's why my blood pressure is high."

As he ranted, I noticed the pattern: every "they" carried the weight of his own anxiety. I asked,

"What happens in your body during these moments?"

He frowned.

"I get headaches. My chest feels tight. I can't breathe sometimes."

We explored further, and slowly he realised: it wasn't only his team—it was his own perfectionism that was suffocating him. The projection dissolved into self-awareness. Resistance had pointed us straight to the real issue.

The Young Bride in Transference

A newly married woman came to me, struggling with constant arguments with her husband. But in session, she often snapped at me:

"You're not listening. You don't care. Just like him!"

It would have been easy to take offence. Instead, I named it gently:

"When you say I don't care, does it feel like I've become your husband in this moment?"

Her eyes widened, then softened.

"Yes… exactly."

For the first time, she recognised that her anger at me was really her anger at him, replayed in the safety of my office. From there, we could work on healthier communication with her husband.

These cases show one thing clearly: resistance is never meaningless. It is a signpost. It tells us where the deepest pain is hiding.

Indian Philosophy: The Ancient Face of Resistance

Resistance is not a modern psychological discovery. Long before counselling rooms existed, Indian philosophical texts described the same inner hesitation—though in different language.

In the *Bhagavad Gita*, the setting is not a temple or a forest—it is a battlefield.

Arjuna, a skilled warrior, stands between two armies. On one side are his cousins and teachers. On the other, his own brothers. The war is about justice, but the cost is unbearable. As he looks at those he must fight, his body weakens. His bow slips from his hand. His mind becomes confused.

He says, in essence:

"I cannot do this. My heart is trembling. My duty feels impossible. I will not fight."

This is resistance in its most human form.

Not laziness.
Not rebellion.
But paralysis born from emotional overwhelm.

Psychologically, Arjuna is experiencing cognitive dissonance, moral conflict, anticipatory grief, and fear. His mind projects catastrophe onto the future. He wants to withdraw—to escape the discomfort.

What is remarkable is Krishna's response.

He does not shame him.
He does not command obedience.
He does not dismiss his fear.

He listens.

He allows Arjuna's confusion to unfold fully. Then, patiently, he reframes the situation—not by denying the difficulty, but by expanding Arjuna's perspective. He guides him from emotional paralysis toward clarity of role, responsibility, and inner steadiness.

Resistance here is not condemned.
It is understood as a necessary stage before insight.

The *Upanishads* present a different but equally powerful illustration.

In the *Katha Upanishad*, a young boy named Nachiketa confronts Yama, the symbolic lord of death. Nachiketa is not paralysed like Arjuna. Instead, he is seeking truth about what lies beyond life.

Yama, testing him, offers distractions:

Wealth.
Pleasure.
Long life.
Power.

But Nachiketa refuses.

He insists on the deeper question:
"What is the truth of existence?"

Here, resistance takes another form.

It is not resistance against duty.
It is resistance against distraction.

From a counselling perspective, both stories illuminate different faces of the human mind:

Arjuna resists moving forward because he is overwhelmed.
Nachiketa resists superficial comfort because he seeks deeper meaning.

In both cases, hesitation precedes growth.

When I explain this to clients—especially those who feel ashamed of their indecision or emotional blocks—I often say gently:

"Your hesitation is not weakness. It is your mind trying to protect you. Just as Arjuna needed time before he could lift his bow, you may need time before you take your next step. And that is alright."

Framed this way, resistance becomes less frightening.

It is no longer proof of failure.

It becomes part of the human process—a pause before alignment, a questioning before commitment, a slowing before movement.

When clients see that even ancient wisdom texts describe confusion, doubt, and inner struggle, their shame softens.

They realise:

"I am not abnormal. I am human."

And that realisation itself becomes therapeutic.

Resistance as a Gateway

Over the years, I have come to see resistance not as an obstacle, but as a companion. When a client resists, they are not saying "I don't want healing." They are saying "I want to be safe as I heal."

Denial shows us where the truth feels unbearable.

Projection shows us where the pain is too heavy to own.

Transference replays old relationships in the counselling room.

And hesitation shows us where identity feels at risk.

Every time I have respected resistance—by waiting, by listening, by reframing—the door has eventually opened. Sometimes slowly, sometimes suddenly, but always with dignity.

Resistance, then, is not a wall to be broken.

It is a gate to be unlocked.

And the key is patience, empathy, and trust.

Key Takeaways & Exercises

Key Takeaways

- Resistance is not opposition—it is protection. Clients resist because change feels risky, unfamiliar, or threatening to identity.
- Denial buys time; it is the mind's way of saying, "I can face only part of the truth now."
- Projection shifts heavy emotions outward; turning the mirror gently inward helps awareness.
- Transference replays old relationships in the counselling room; if addressed gently, it can lead to deep healing.
- Techniques to soften resistance include metaphor, pacing, reframing, and humour.
- Indian philosophy (Arjuna in the Gita, Nachiketa in the Katha Upanishad) reminds us that hesitation is part of the journey, not a flaw.
- Resistance is not a wall—it is a gate. The counsellor's role is to wait patiently and help the client find the key.

Practical Exercises

1. Mirror Exercise: Recall a time when you blamed others strongly. Ask: *What was I really feeling inside my body?* Write it down. Notice if projection was at play.
2. Denial Journal: Think of a situation where you said "I'm fine" but weren't. Write what truth felt too heavy at that time. Reflect on how denial protected you.
3. Role-play transference: Imagine speaking to someone who frustrates you. Then switch roles and answer as them. Notice if similar emotions arise with people in your present life.
4. Metaphor Practice: Think of a difficult area in your life as a locked room. Write what might be inside, and what kind of "lamp" (support, skill, ritual) you'd need to enter safely.
5. Gentle Humour: When feeling stuck, write down a humorous reframe of the problem (e.g., "My boss doesn't give me stress; he gives me cardio practice!"). Laughter often melts resistance.

CHAPTER 9

SELF-CARE FOR COUNSELLORS

The Night of Too Many Calls

It was the third week of the lockdown. My phone had not stopped ringing for days. People from across the country were calling - panic in their voices, fear of death in their words. Some were gasping, others sobbing, some whispering so their families wouldn't hear.

That night, I took nearly twenty calls back-to-back. Each person wanted reassurance:

"Will I survive?"

"What if I infect my children?"

"Why is this happening to us?"

I listened, calmed, guided, sometimes prayed with them. By 3 a.m., my throat was dry, my body heavy, my own chest tight with borrowed fear.

When I finally put the phone down, I realised: I had absorbed the pain of hundreds but given no thought to my own. The healer had become the vessel of too much sorrow.

That night taught me something vital: a counsellor who forgets to care for themselves cannot care well for others.

The Hidden Cost of Caring

To the outside world, counselling looks calm. A professional sits in a chair, listening, nodding, occasionally asking questions. It seems effortless.

But anyone who has sat in that chair knows: it is sacred labour.

You are not just hearing words—you are absorbing grief, fear, shame, rage.

Every counsellor, knowingly or unknowingly, carries fragments of their clients' pain home with them.

- A widow's cry may echo in your dreams.
- A teenager's despair may shadow your own mood.
- A corporate leader's anger may leave your shoulders tense long after the session.
- A child's fear of school may make you worry about your own children.

This is the hidden cost of caring: compassion fatigue.

It doesn't arrive suddenly. It creeps in quietly, like slow water, until one day you realise you are exhausted, irritable, or emotionally numb.

I have seen fellow counsellors burn out silently. They push themselves to be endlessly available, answering late-night calls, taking extra sessions, carrying guilt if they say no. Eventually, some lose the joy of the work itself. They become counsellors in body but not in spirit.

A Story of Blurred Boundaries

I recall a fellow professional who prided herself on being "always there" for her clients. She gave out her personal number, answered messages at midnight, and agreed to extra sessions on Sundays.

At first, her clients adored her. But slowly, she grew resentful.

She confided to me once:

"I feel like their servant, not their counsellor."

What had happened?

Her boundaries had blurred. By forgetting her own needs, she had trained her clients to believe she was endlessly available. When she finally tried to reclaim her time, they felt abandoned. Both sides suffered.

This story is not unusual. Many of us enter this profession with big hearts. We want to heal everyone. But if our compassion is not balanced with self-care, it turns from healing to harm—for both client and counsellor.

The Body Keeps the Score

Modern neuroscience confirms what experienced counsellors have long sensed intuitively: the body records stress and emotional trauma, even when the mind tries to move on.

Ground-breaking work by Bessel van der Kolk, particularly in his seminal book *The Body Keeps the Score*, demonstrates that traumatic experiences are stored not only as memories but as physiological imprints—in muscle tension, breathing patterns, hormonal responses, and the nervous system itself. Trauma, he explains, reorganises how the brain and body respond to stress.

Research has also shown that trauma does not affect only those who directly experience it. Mental-health professionals who listen deeply to accounts of suffering may themselves absorb emotional and somatic residues of that pain—a phenomenon known as vicarious trauma or secondary traumatic stress. Studies indicate that counsellors exposed repeatedly to clients' traumatic narratives may develop symptoms such as intrusive imagery, disturbed sleep, emotional numbing, and heightened anxiety.

I remember a period when several of my clients were survivors of domestic violence. Night after night, I found myself dreaming of locked rooms and angry voices. Though those events were not mine, my subconscious had absorbed them. My nervous system had registered their fear and helplessness. My body was, quite literally, *keeping the score.*

This is why self-care is not a luxury for counsellors—it is a professional necessity and a form of psychological hygiene.

Just as a surgeon sterilises instruments to prevent infection, a counsellor must regularly cleanse and regulate their inner emotional space—through supervision, reflection, rest, grounding practices, and emotional release—so that healing work does not quietly turn into hidden harm.

There is a saying among counsellors:

"You cannot be your own mirror."

Even the most seasoned professional cannot always see their blind spots. That is why supervision—sharing one's work with another experienced counsellor—is essential.

Early in my career, after a session with a grieving father, I felt unusually heavy. I carried his sorrow into the next session, then into the evening.

A senior colleague noticed and said:

"You're still sitting with the father, aren't you?"

Her words startled me. She was right.

In supervision, I unpacked what happened—my own unresolved grief for a relative had resonated with his. Without that mirror, I might have drowned silently in borrowed sorrow.

Supervision is not judgment. It is a safe dialogue where counsellors can admit mistakes, express frustrations, even cry if needed.

In some cultures, it is neglected, seen as weakness. But in truth, it is strength. Just as doctors consult peers for complex cases, counsellors must seek mirrors for their inner world.

Rituals of Cleansing: Closing the Session Properly

After each session, I have a small ritual. I sit for a minute, close my eyes, and take three slow breaths.

As I exhale, I imagine returning the client's emotions to them with respect:

"This is your journey, not mine.

May you find healing.

May I remain steady."

This simple practice acts like washing hands after surgery.

Without it, emotions linger.

With it, I feel lighter.

Even in busy days with back-to-back sessions, this one-minute pause protects my inner space.

Rituals need not be religious. They can be:

- Lighting incense
- Writing a few lines in a journal
- Walking silently for five minutes
- Listening to calming music

The act itself signals to the subconscious:

"This story is complete for now. You may rest."

Boundaries: The Fence that Protects the Garden

A counsellor without boundaries is like a garden without a fence—beautiful for a while, until animals trample the flowers.

I once worked with a client who texted me daily, sometimes five or six times. At first, I replied kindly. But soon, my evenings were filled with her messages, and resentment grew.

I realised I had failed her as much as myself.

The next session, I said gently:

"I care for you deeply, but I can only respond during our scheduled sessions. Between sessions, I encourage you to use the tools we practised."

She frowned. Even protested.

But over time, she learnt to trust herself more.

Setting that boundary did not harm her progress—it strengthened it.

And it saved my energy.

Boundaries are not rejection.

They are structure.

Self-Care Across Different Counselling Domains

Over the years, I have learnt that self-care does not look the same across all forms of counselling. Each domain carries its own emotional weight, its own unseen residue. What nourishes the counsellor in one area may not be sufficient in another. Awareness of this difference itself becomes an act of self-care.

Marital Counselling

After intense couples sessions—where the room is filled with accusation, grief, disappointment, and years of unresolved conflict—I noticed how easily that emotional charge lingered within me. Early in my practice, I sometimes carried that tension home, finding myself unusually irritable or withdrawn with my own family.

I learnt, with experience, that before re-entering my personal space, I needed grounding. A few minutes of silence, conscious breathing, or even a brief walk helped me reset. Without this pause, the echoes of another couple's pain risked spilling into my own relationships. Self-care here meant *emotional transition*—closing one world before stepping into another.

Child Counselling

Working with children touches a very tender place. Listening to their fears—of bullying, exams, parental conflict, or loneliness—often stirred my own parental instincts and anxieties. Some stories stayed with me long after the session ended.

I realised that unless I consciously released these emotions, I began to carry unnecessary worry into my home and family life. I learnt to gently remind myself: *This child is safe now. I have done my part.* Letting go became an essential skill, not a sign of indifference, but of psychological hygiene.

Corporate Counselling

Corporate settings present a different challenge altogether. After sessions with aggressive, highly driven leaders—where control, dominance, and pressure dominate the conversation—I sometimes noticed my own voice becoming firmer, my patience thinner.

Self-awareness became my safeguard. Simply recognising the shift in my tone was enough to soften it. A counsellor must not unconsciously absorb the emotional posture of the corporate world. Self-care here meant *returning to my natural rhythm*—restoring calm, balance, and warmth.

Addiction Recovery

Walking alongside individuals struggling with addiction demands deep emotional endurance. Relapse, despair, guilt, and repeated setbacks can quietly erode the counsellor's optimism. There were moments when I felt drained—not because of failure, but because of prolonged exposure to suffering.

In this domain, supervision was not optional; it was my anchor. Speaking openly with peers helped me process my own feelings of helplessness and frustration. Self-care here meant *shared reflection*—remembering that no counsellor heals alone.

Career Confusion

Young adults torn between passion and pressure often awakened memories of my own early struggles—choices, uncertainty, expectations. Without awareness, their dilemmas could blur into my own past.

I learnt to consciously separate their journey from mine. Their confusion deserved empathy, not projection. Self-care in this space meant *clear emotional boundaries*—offering guidance without reliving my own story.

Each counselling domain leaves a different emotional imprint. Recognising this diversity is crucial. Self-care is not indulgence; it is the only shield that allows the counsellor to remain present without becoming burdened.

Finding Joy Beyond the Counselling Room

Self-care is not only about avoiding burnout.

It is also about nurturing joy.

There were phases in my career when I immersed myself so completely in clients' struggles that I forgot my own sources of renewal. Music was postponed. Walks were skipped. Friendships were delayed. Slowly, without realising it, I began to function more mechanically, with less inner vitality.

One day, while absent-mindedly humming an old Malayalam song I loved, I felt a quiet spark return. Something inside softened. In that moment, I understood a simple truth:

Joy is not selfish—it is fuel.

Since then, I have consciously protected my joy.

Music that soothes.

Nature walks that ground.

Poetry that reflects.

Painting that absorbs.

Laughter shared with friends.

These moments do not distract me from my work; they prepare me for it. They refill the inner reservoir from which empathy flows. A counsellor who nurtures joy does not become less serious—only more human.

Indian Wisdom: Balance as Dharma

Indian wisdom has always cautioned against extremes. Long before burnout became a clinical term, imbalance was recognised as a quiet destroyer of clarity and strength.

The *Bhagavad Gita* offers a striking reminder:

"Yoga is not for one who eats too much,

nor for one who eats too little,

nor for one who sleeps too much,

nor for one who sleeps too little."

(Bhagavad Gita, 6:16)

Though spoken in a spiritual context, this verse speaks directly to counsellors. It reminds us that imbalance—whether in work, sacrifice, or neglect—

gradually erodes harmony. Overwork dulls sensitivity. Over-sacrifice breeds resentment. Neglect of the body clouds the mind.

The *Upanishads* deepen this understanding through the concept of samyama—discipline held in harmony. Samyama is not harsh control; it is intelligent restraint guided by self-awareness.

For counsellors, samyama means knowing when to give and when to pause.

It means honouring the body that listens, the mind that holds stories, and the nervous system that absorbs emotional charge.

It means allowing rest without guilt, recognising that restoration is not weakness but wisdom.

In this sense, self-care is not separate from ethical practice. It is woven into the very discipline of counselling.

When the Counsellor Nearly Breaks

Years ago, there was a period when my calendar was packed beyond reason. From early morning until late evening, session followed session. And when the day ended, the phone continued to ring—late-night calls, urgent voices, unspoken desperation.

One evening, after a particularly long day, I returned home and sat at the dining table. Food was placed before me, but I could not eat. My family spoke, yet their words did not reach me. My mind was still occupied elsewhere—replaying the day's voices: a widow's sobbing, a teenager's panic, a businessman's rage.

That night, I dreamt of drowning.

Not in water—but in words.

Voices calling out, overlapping, pulling me under.

I woke up shaken, but clear.

If I continued this way, I realised, I would soon become the one needing counselling.

That moment became my turning point.

At first, change felt uncomfortable. Saying "no" felt selfish. Setting limits felt unkind. Taking rest felt lazy. But slowly, with reflection and humility, I learned a truth that experience alone can teach:

Self-care is not the opposite of service.

It is the foundation of it.

Without rest, presence fades. Without boundaries, compassion turns brittle. Without renewal, even the sincerest counsellor begins to function mechanically rather than mindfully.

The Counsellor as Human

There is a quiet myth surrounding this profession—that counsellors are somehow superhuman. Calm at all times. Wise in every situation. Endlessly patient and emotionally untouched.

But counsellors are human.

We feel anger.

We experience doubt.

We grow tired.

We worry about our families.

We have our own unresolved moments.

Clients sometimes place us on pedestals, believing we must never falter. But pedestals are dangerous places to stand. They deny reality, and they invite collapse.

The most effective counsellors I know are not those who deny their humanity, but those who accept it with honesty. They can say, without shame:

"I struggle too—and that is why I understand the importance of these tools."

Their authenticity does not weaken their work; it strengthens it. By managing their humanity wisely, they ensure it does not spill into the client's healing space.

Self-Care as Dharma

In the Indian tradition, dharma means duty—but never a duty that excludes oneself. A counsellor's dharma is twofold:

- To serve others with integrity
- To preserve the self that serves

Neglect either, and imbalance follows.

Self-care, then, is not optional. It is dharmic. It sustains clarity, steadiness, and compassion over time. It allows the counsellor to enter the counselling space with lightness rather than weariness, with openness rather than quiet depletion.

Over five decades of practice, I have learned this lesson repeatedly, sometimes gently, sometimes through exhaustion. The counsellor who honours their own needs does not become less effective—only more so. Their steadiness itself becomes healing. Their balance reassures. Their presence calms.

In the end, caring for the self is not a retreat from responsibility.

It is a commitment to practise counselling with longevity, dignity, and grace.

Key Takeaways & Exercises

Key Takeaways

- Counsellors carry invisible burdens—vicarious trauma, compassion fatigue.
- Supervision provides a mirror for blind spots.
- Small rituals help release emotional residue.
- Boundaries protect both client and counsellor.
- Joy is fuel, not indulgence.
- Indian wisdom teaches balance as dharma.
- Self-care is duty, not selfishness.

Practical Exercises

1. Closing Ritual:
2. After a heavy conversation, pause and whisper:
3. "This is not mine to carry."
4. Boundary Reflection:
5. Write one area you feel overstretched.
6. Design a gentle boundary.
7. Joy Journal:
8. Note one joyful act daily.
9. Peer Check-In:
10. Speak with a colleague about your emotional load.
11. Balance Audit:
12. Track sleep, food, rest, and work for one week.
13. Ask:
14. "Am I walking the middle path?"

CHAPTER 10

COUNSELLING IN SPECIAL CONTEXTS

One Size Never Fits All

If earlier chapters explored what counselling is, this chapter shows how those principles come alive when contexts change.

Counselling is often imagined as a quiet room with two chairs, a counsellor, and a client. But life does not happen in tidy rooms. Problems spill over into schools, workplaces, families, and hospital corridors. If the counsellor insists on one rigid format, they will miss half the opportunities to heal. True counselling is like water—it takes the shape of the vessel it enters.

I first realised this in a school many years ago. A teacher called me in.

"One of our brightest students has stopped attending classes. Please talk to her."

I found the girl sitting alone in the playground, scribbling circles in the sand. When I sat beside her, she didn't look up. Finally, she whispered,

"I'm useless. Everyone thinks I'm stupid now."

Her grades had slipped after her parents' divorce, and the whispers of classmates had become knives. In that moment, she didn't need a lecture on resilience or a clinical explanation of stress. She needed someone to sit on the dusty ground with her and see her pain without judgement.

We spoke about her favourite subject—biology. I asked her to explain photosynthesis to me. Her eyes lit up as she taught me. By the end of that short talk, she murmured,

"Maybe I'm not useless after all."

That was counselling in a school context—not a formal session, but a moment of human connection where hope was restored.

School and Adolescent Counselling: A Battlefield of Identities

Adolescence is often described as a storm—and rightly so. Identity, independence, peer pressure, academic stress—all clash like thunderclouds. For many students, school becomes less of a classroom and more of a battlefield where they are constantly judged.

I once counselled Rohan, a 15-year-old who had suddenly turned disruptive in class. Teachers labelled him "arrogant," classmates mocked him, and his parents feared he was "going astray."

But beneath the sarcasm lay a painful truth: he had failed mathematics for the first time. His arrogance was not rebellion—it was armour.

Knowing his love for cricket, I reframed his struggle.

"When a batsman is bowled out," I asked, "does that end his career?"

He smiled. "No, sir. He learns and faces the next ball."

That metaphor became his anchor. Remedial classes turned into "net practice." Slowly, confidence returned.

The Role of the Counsellor in Schools

Children rarely arrive with labels for their inner pain. They may not say "I am depressed" or "I am anxious," but their distress speaks in other languages—through long silences, angry outbursts, fading curiosity, withdrawn drawings, or sudden changes in behaviour. What appears as mischief or defiance is often a wordless plea to be understood.

Adolescents, in particular, resist direct advice. Instructions feel like control, and lectures feel like judgment. Yet the same adolescents listen closely to stories, humour, and metaphors—because these invite reflection without confrontation. A well-told story can reach where advice is instantly rejected.

Within a school, the counsellor therefore wears many roles. At times, the counsellor is a **guide**, offering skills to cope with stress and confusion. At other moments, a **bridge**, gently translating between the worlds of students, parents, and teachers. And often, a **mirror**, helping young people see strengths and possibilities they cannot yet recognise in themselves.

Above all, the counsellor must be a **safe presence**—someone who does not rush to correct, label, or fix. When a teenager says, *"I hate everyone,"* what they are often asking is something far more vulnerable:

"Does anyone really see me, and will I be accepted if they do?"

A Reflection from Indian Wisdom

Indian psychology does not present a rigid doctrine meant to be applied uniformly to every person. Instead, it offers contextual wisdom—guidance shaped by age, temperament, stage of life, and inner readiness. What nourishes a child does not necessarily guide an adolescent. What steadies an adult may overwhelm a young mind. Centuries before developmental psychology became a formal discipline, Indian thought recognised that human growth unfolds in stages, and guidance must evolve accordingly.

This sensitivity to stage and readiness is beautifully reflected in the ancient *gurukul* tradition. Education was not confined to textbooks or examinations. A student lived in close proximity to the guru, observing how he spoke, how he ate, how he responded to difficulty. Learning happened through shared daily life—through dialogue under trees, through silence at dawn, through questions asked at the right moment.

The aim was not merely to transfer information, but to awaken discernment—what Indian philosophy calls *viveka*, the ability to distinguish between impulse and insight, reaction and wisdom.

The Upanishads capture this spirit through living conversations rather than lectures. Consider the dialogue between the young seeker Nachiketa and Yama, or between Svetaketu and his father Uddalaka. The teacher does not dictate conclusions. Instead, he asks:

"Have you understood that by knowing one thing, everything else becomes known?"
"Who are you, truly—beyond name and role?"
"What remains when everything external changes?"

These are not questions meant to impress; they are meant to provoke inward reflection. Insight arises not because the teacher supplies answers, but because the student is guided to see for himself.

This approach is deeply relevant to adolescent counselling.

A teenager struggling with identity rarely responds well to direct instruction. If we say, "You should not worry about what others think," the words often bounce off resistance. But if we ask gently, "When do you feel most like yourself?" or "What matters to you beyond others' opinions?" something shifts. The question opens a door the lecture cannot.

I once worked with a 16-year-old who constantly compared himself to classmates. His self-esteem fluctuated with every exam result and every social media post. Instead of reassuring him repeatedly, I asked:

"When was the last time you did something and forgot to compare yourself with anyone?"

He paused for a long time before replying, "When I was sketching alone."

That moment became his turning point. The discovery was his—not imposed by me. And because it was discovered, not delivered, it stayed.

Indian wisdom understood this long ago: what is realised inwardly becomes stable; what is imposed externally often fades.

In counselling adolescents, therefore, we do not aim to provide ready-made solutions. We create a reflective space—through stories, metaphors, questions, and patient listening—where young people can encounter their own clarity.

And what emerges from within does not require constant reinforcement. It settles quietly. It strengthens over time. It becomes part of identity.

Just as the guru did not force insight but awakened it, the counsellor does not impose maturity—but invites it.

The Living Room Battlefield

Family quarrels rarely look like epic battles. They are fought in ordinary spaces—over dinner plates, over forgotten birthdays, over who didn't switch off the light. Yet beneath these trivial sparks burn deeper fires of unmet needs and unspoken hurts.

Sunil and Meera walked into my counselling room carrying this invisible fire. Sunil's jaw was tight, his arms folded. Meera's eyes were tired, her voice sharp.

"She doesn't respect me," Sunil burst out. *"Whatever I say, she argues."*

Meera snapped back: *"Respect? How can I respect someone who never listens? He just wants everything his way."*

Their words collided like cymbals in an angry orchestra. If I had let them, they would have replayed this quarrel endlessly. Instead, I held up a hand. *"Let's pause. Not to stop you from speaking—but to hear what lies beneath these words."*

Over time, I learnt that Sunil grew up in a household where men's words were final, unquestionable. Meera, on the other hand, was raised in a home where women debated fiercely and openly. What looked like "disrespect" was not malice. It was two histories, two traditions, colliding in the present.

One day, I interrupted their quarrel with an unusual request. *"Sunil, tell Meera one thing you admire in her. Only one. No arguments, no conditions."*

He hesitated, then muttered, *"She's a good mother."*

I turned to Meera. *"And you—tell him one thing you value."*

She sighed, then whispered: *"He works hard for us. He does provide."*

The silence that followed was different. Softer. In that tiny moment, admiration pierced through accusation. They still fought, yes - but they also began to remember why they had chosen each other in the first place. That moment of remembering became the seed of healing.

Marital counselling is not about erasing arguments—it is about teaching couples to listen beneath the noise, to find the music they once danced to.

Parents and Children: Two Generations, Two Languages

In family counselling, parents and children often feel like they live on different planets. One speaks the language of discipline and responsibility; the other speaks the language of freedom and belonging.

Aditya, a 13-year-old boy, embodied this clash. His parents arrived first, distraught.

"He is addicted to video games. He locks himself in. He won't talk to us anymore," they said, their voices heavy with disappointment.

When I sat with Aditya alone, he slouched in his chair, hoodie pulled over his head. I asked gently,

"What do these games give you?"

For the first time, he lifted his eyes.

"When I play, I feel strong. Outside… I feel small. They don't get it."

His parents saw laziness. He saw survival.

In the joint session, I acted as translator. To the parents, I said:

"For him, the game is not just a toy—it is a place where he feels powerful, in control. That's why it matters."

To Aditya, I said:

"Your parents are not your enemies. They're scared. They miss the boy who used to talk to them."

The air shifted. His mother asked softly,

"Can we play with you once? Just to see?"

His face lit up with surprise. They began a weekly ritual: Friday night gaming together. At the same time, Aditya agreed to limit his hours and spend more evenings at the dining table.

The result was not just reduced screen time.

It was a bridge built across two languages.

The Counsellor's Role in Family Healing

In these sessions, I often feel less like a doctor and more like a conductor in an orchestra. Each family member plays a different instrument—too loud, too soft, sometimes painfully out of tune. My role is not to replace the music, but to help them listen to one another until harmony slowly returns.

This often means guiding small but powerful shifts. Instead of saying, "You never listen," I invite them to try, "I feel unheard." The truth remains the same—but without poison.

At times, I stop a session mid-sentence and say gently,

"Can you repeat that—without the word *always*?"

The change is immediate. The room breathes again.

I may also ask them to recall a shared moment of joy before discussing pain. When love is remembered, anger softens.

These moments may seem minor, but they ripple outward. A softened tone at the counselling table becomes a softened tone at breakfast. A shared laugh in session becomes a shared laugh in the kitchen. Healing is not dramatic—it is daily.

Indian Wisdom: Family as Sacred Ground

In the Indian worldview, the family is not merely a social unit—it is a sacred arena where the deepest lessons of life are learnt.

The ancient concept of ashramas, or stages of life, placed grihastha—the stage of householding—at the very heart of dharma. One may meditate in forests or debate in royal courts, but it is within the family that patience, compassion, sacrifice, and forgiveness are tested every day.

The *Mahabharata* reminds us that even the greatest figures could not escape family conflict. Yudhishthira, the embodiment of truth, gambled away everything he loved. Bhishma, bound by vows, watched helplessly as his family collapsed. Draupadi's cry for justice arose not from strangers, but from her own kin.

These stories endure because they echo every household: divided loyalties, unspoken wounds, the tension between love and pride.

What do these epics teach us? That conflict within families is not failure—it is the natural arena where human strengths and weaknesses collide. Just as Kurukshetra became the ground where Arjuna learnt the deepest truths of life, today's dining tables, bedrooms, and living rooms are where patience and empathy are practised.

The *Bhagavad Gita* reminds us that running away from one's duty does not bring peace. In family life, avoidance—through silence, withdrawal, or blame—only deepens wounds. Facing conflict with awareness, guided by love, is the path of dharma.

The *Upanishads* offer a gentler metaphor: the family as a yajna, a sacred fire. Each member must offer something—time, care, respect, restraint. If one withholds, the fire dims. When all contribute, the family glows.

I often tell families:

"Your home is your Kurukshetra and your yajna at once. Winning arguments is not victory. Sustaining love is."

Modern psychology speaks of the family as a system—each action ripples through all members. Indian wisdom spoke of this truth centuries ago. Nothing in a family happens in isolation.

To remind families of this is to lift them from guilt into perspective. Quarrels become opportunities—for forgiveness, for rediscovering admiration, for remembering that love is larger than ego.

As I often say:

"Your greatest temple is not outside—it is your home. Your prayers are the daily acts of patience, apology, and kindness you offer one another."

Workplace & Corporate Counselling

The Office as a Theatre of Minds

At first glance, the workplace appears to be a world of logic and efficiency—desks aligned in neat rows, reports submitted on time, meetings governed by agendas and deadlines. Yet beneath this orderly surface lies a far more complex reality. Every office is a theatre of human minds.

Behind each designation—manager, assistant, executive—stands a person shaped by past successes and old failures, carrying private fears, unspoken ambitions, and invisible emotional wounds. When these inner stories remain unheard, they quietly spill into performance, relationships, and health. Productivity drops, conflicts multiply, and stress becomes contagious.

Counselling in the workplace is not about diagnosing disorders or labelling behaviour. It is about restoring understanding and humanity, so people can work not just efficiently, but sanely.

The Angry Supervisor

Raghav walked into the counselling room with confidence and irritation in equal measure. His record spoke for itself—targets met, deadlines enforced, results delivered. Yet complaints followed him everywhere.

"They are lazy, ungrateful, and careless," he said bluntly. "If I don't shout, nothing moves."

As he spoke, his voice rose automatically, as if volume itself were proof of authority.

As we explored his history, a different picture emerged. Raghav had grown up in a home where mistakes were met with harsh words and raised voices. Correction had always come wrapped in fear. In his mind, shouting was not cruelty—it was responsibility.

Instead of confronting him directly, I chose a language he loved: cricket.

"You're bowling bouncers all the time," I said. "No batsman plays well when every ball is aimed at his head. What happens if you bowl a slower ball occasionally—or acknowledge a good shot?"

He laughed at first, then fell silent.

Over the next few weeks, he experimented. Meetings began with appreciation instead of criticism. Firmness remained, but it was no longer laced with humiliation. Gradually, the atmosphere shifted. His team stopped flinching and started contributing.

Discipline did not disappear—but fear loosened its grip. Raghav had not lost authority; he had gained leadership.

The Silent Employee

Not all workplace struggles announce themselves loudly. Some hide in silence.

Priya had been flagged by her manager for declining performance. She avoided eye contact in meetings, spoke rarely, and submitted reports late. The assumption was simple: disengagement.

When she finally spoke in session, her voice trembled.

"Every time I think of speaking in a meeting," she said, "I hear my old teacher's voice saying, 'You'll never amount to anything.' My mind goes blank."

This was not a problem of competence. It was a wound of memory.

Together, we worked gently. When the inner critic whispered failure, she practised responding with a quieter, kinder truth: *I am learning. Learning is not failure.* Before meetings, she grounded herself—feet firm on the floor, breath steady, recalling moments when she had succeeded.

The change was gradual, not dramatic. But it was real. She began to speak. Her ideas surfaced. Her confidence returned.

Later, her manager told me, almost in disbelief,

"She's one of our strongest thinkers. I can't believe we nearly lost her."

Sometimes, counselling does not just heal people—it saves organisations from losing their best minds.

The Stress of Leadership

Leadership carries a burden few openly acknowledge. One senior executive once confessed,

"Everyone thinks I'm confident. But every night, I lie awake asking myself—what if I make the wrong decision and hundreds of people suffer?"

For him, leadership meant isolation. He could not share his doubts with his board, his employees, or even his family. He feared that admitting uncertainty would erode trust.

In counselling, we worked on separating decision-making from self-worth. A decision, I reminded him, is an action—not a verdict on one's value. We explored how even incorrect decisions often lead to learning, adaptation, and growth.

Through therapeutic meditation, he learned to steady his mind before high-pressure meetings—anchoring himself in breath and clarity rather than fear.

Over time, his inner image changed. He stopped seeing himself as a man balancing a fragile tower, terrified of collapse. Instead, he began to see himself as a sailor—adjusting sails, reading winds, knowing that storms are part of the journey, not signs of failure.

Leadership became lighter, not because responsibility vanished, but because fear no longer ruled it.

Indian Wisdom: The Workplace as Karma-Bhumi

Indian philosophy invites us to see work not merely as obligation or pressure, but as karma-bhumi—the field of conscious action. Work, in this view, is not separate from inner life; it is one of its most active expressions.

The *Bhagavad Gita* offers a deceptively simple teaching: perform your duty with sincerity, but do not drown in anxiety about outcomes. When effort becomes chained to fear of results, work turns into a burden. When effort is offered with awareness and integrity, work becomes meaningful—even transformative.

In modern workplaces, stress rarely comes from the task itself. It arises from the relentless loop of *What if I fail? What will they think? What if this costs me everything?* When professionals begin to internalise the Gita's wisdom—focusing on preparation, clarity, and effort rather than constant self-judgement—something subtle but powerful shifts.

Workplaces soften. Leaders inspire without dominating. Employees engage without burning out. Productivity no longer feels like extraction, but like participation. Karma-bhumi becomes not a battlefield, but a space for purposeful action.

Crisis Counselling & Closing Reflections

When Crisis Strikes

Crisis counselling stands apart from all other forms of counselling. In ordinary settings, there is time—time to listen, to explore, to understand. In crisis, time collapses. The person is already at the edge, overwhelmed by fear, grief, or panic.

Here, counselling is no longer about interpretation or insight. It becomes an anchor—steadying the inner storm when the outer one cannot be controlled. The counsellor's presence itself becomes the intervention.

The Man Who Couldn't Breathe

Panic rarely announces itself politely. It rushes in ahead of reason, tightening the chest, scattering thought, convincing the body that danger is immediate and overwhelming. In such moments, the mind struggles to keep pace, and the body takes command.

During one such call, breath had turned shallow and frantic, each gasp feeding the next wave of fear. Words came in broken fragments. We did not argue with the panic; we slowed it. Through deliberate, steady breathing and the quiet rhythm of a calm voice, the body was gently reminded that it was still safe enough to breathe.

Breath by breath, the noise of panic softened. Control returned—not all at once, but gradually. The crisis did not disappear, but something essential was restored: the ability to remain present without collapsing. And that is where survival truly begins.

The Young Widow's Call

In the raw aftermath of loss, the mind rejects logic. Words meant to console fall flat, and the future feels not distant but impossible. Grief collapses time, leaving the person trapped in an endless present of pain.

When she spoke, her voice was unsteady, breaking between sobs.

"I can't live like this," she whispered. "There is nothing left to look forward to."

In such moments, counselling deliberately becomes small. We do not speak of healing, recovery, or hope—those words belong to another day. Instead, we stay with what is bearable now. I asked her to breathe with me, just for this moment. Not tomorrow. Not the weeks ahead. Only this minute.

Minute by minute, the intensity softened—not because the pain disappeared, but because she was no longer alone inside it. Together, we held time in fragments small enough to survive.

Crisis counselling in grief does not mend what has been lost. It does something more urgent: it protects life itself, quietly holding the person steady until strength can begin, slowly, to return.

Crisis Counselling in Medical Settings

In emergency wards and intensive care units, fear often becomes a second, invisible illness—one that does not show up on scans or blood reports, yet powerfully shapes recovery. The beeping monitors, hurried footsteps, masked faces, and unfamiliar machines can overwhelm even the strongest mind. For many patients, especially those facing sudden or life-threatening conditions, the body may be stabilised while the mind remains in crisis.

I recall one such case of a man recovering from major cardiac surgery. Medically, his condition was stable. The surgeons were satisfied, the vitals were within range, and the treatment plan was clear. Yet something was not moving forward. He was restless, breathing irregularly, unable to sleep, and repeatedly pressing the call bell. Nurses described him as "uncooperative," but what I heard beneath that label was fear.

When I spoke to him, his words came in short bursts:

"What if my heart stops again?"
"What if I don't wake up?"
"I feel like I'm losing control."

This was not a medical complication—it was a psychological emergency.

Brief crisis counselling focused first on calming his nervous system. We worked gently with breath regulation, slowing the exhalation to signal safety to the body. I reassured him in simple, grounded language, explaining what each sensation meant and what was already being managed by the medical team. I then guided him through mild imagery—inviting him to picture his heart not as fragile, but as supported, watched over, and steadily healing.

As his fear softened, subtle changes followed. His breathing became more rhythmic. His muscles relaxed. He began sleeping in short but restorative intervals. Most importantly, he started cooperating with physiotherapy and nursing care. The same body that had resisted recovery under fear now responded once calm returned.

This was not counselling replacing medicine.

It was counselling *supporting* medicine—removing fear as an obstacle to healing.

In medical settings, this distinction is crucial. When fear dominates, it activates stress hormones that interfere with immunity, healing, and compliance. When fear is addressed, the body's natural capacity to recover re-emerges. Crisis counselling, even when brief, ensures that psychological distress does not sabotage medical progress.

For counsellors working alongside doctors and nurses, this role carries responsibility—and also demands self-care. Bearing witness to suffering in such intense environments requires clarity, emotional grounding, and strong inner boundaries. Only a counsellor who is regulated within themselves can help regulate another in crisis.

The Flooded House on the Terrace (Kerala Floods)

Crisis does not always arrive as illness. Sometimes, it arrives as water—relentless, rising, swallowing everything familiar.

During the devastating floods in Kerala, I received calls from families trapped in their homes, forced upward floor by floor until there was nowhere left to go but the terrace. Electricity had failed. Food was gone. The roar of water drowned even their own thoughts. What remained was fear—raw and overwhelming.

One such call stays with me. A woman stood on the terrace with her children, clutching her phone as the water surged below. Her voice trembled as she said,

"There is no way out. We will die here."

I could not stop the floodwaters. I could not send rescue boats faster. All I could offer was presence.

I asked her to hold her children's hands and breathe with me. I spoke slowly, guiding her to imagine a steady light above them—unchanging, protective—while the water raged beneath. As she repeated the words, her sobbing eased. The children grew quiet, pressing closer to her. Fear loosened its grip, just enough.

The storm did not stop. But panic did.

For that hour, while the water continued to rise, their minds remained afloat. When rescue finally arrived, she called again—not to say thank you for saving their lives, but for helping them stay sane until help came.

Crisis counselling does not remove the storm.

It helps the mind endure until the storm passes.

Reflections from Indian Wisdom

Indian wisdom reminds us that crisis is not an interruption to life—it is one of its most revealing moments. The *Bhagavad Gita* itself opens on a battlefield, with Arjuna paralysed by fear, his body trembling and his mind clouded. His collapse is not portrayed as weakness, but as the necessary pause before understanding can arise.

The *Upanishads* offer a gentler image. They remind us that when the river swells and currents grow fierce, we may not have the power to calm the waters. What we do have is the ability to steady the boat. In moments of crisis, survival often depends not on changing circumstances, but on stabilising the inner state.

Seen this way, crisis is not a detour from the human journey. It is life itself—concentrated, urgent, stripped of distractions. And when met with guidance and awareness, even the most frightening moments can become gateways to inner strength.

The Counsellor as Anchor in Storms

Across schools, families, workplaces, and disasters, counselling travels wherever suffering exists.

In moments of crisis, the counsellor is not a saviour—but an anchor.

The most healing words are not explanations or answers, but simple companionship:

"I am here. You are not alone."

Key Takeaways

- Counselling changes shape with context.
- Whether in a school, a family, a workplace, or a disaster zone, the heart of counselling remains the same—but its form must adapt. One size never fits all.
- In crises, time becomes small.
- Crisis counselling is not about long-term insight or solutions. It is about stabilising emotions *now*—helping a person survive this minute, then the next.
- Breath is often the first doorway back to safety.
- When panic overwhelms the mind, the body must be calmed first. Slow, steady breathing—guided by a calm voice—can interrupt fear and restore a sense of control.
- Presence matters more than answers.
- In grief and despair, explanations and reassurances often fail. What sustains people is companionship—knowing someone is with them, without judgement or urgency.
- Imagination can protect the mind when the body is trapped.
- In situations where escape is impossible—hospital beds, flooded homes, locked-down environments—guided imagery can prevent panic from becoming overwhelming.
- Counselling and medicine work best together.

- A calm mind supports the body's capacity to heal. Counselling does not replace medical care; it strengthens it by ensuring fear does not sabotage recovery.
- Families, workplaces, and schools are emotional systems.
- No behaviour exists in isolation. When one person's tone softens, another's resistance eases. Small shifts ripple outward and change the entire environment.
- Indian wisdom reinforces modern psychology.
- From Arjuna's paralysis to the metaphor of steadying the boat, ancient texts remind us that crisis is not failure—it is part of the human journey, demanding awareness and guidance.
- The counsellor's role is to be an anchor, not a rescuer.
- Counsellors do not remove storms. They help people remain steady within them—until strength returns and the storm passes.

CHAPTER 11

LEGAL ISSUES, PRECAUTIONS, AND SAFETY MEASURES FOR COUNSELLORS

The Unspoken Risk

A counsellor's room is meant to be a sanctuary—a place where people speak what they have never dared to say aloud. It is designed for trust, vulnerability, and healing. Yet few counsellors are prepared for an uncomfortable truth: the same space of healing can, at times, become a space of misunderstanding or accusation.

I once heard of a young counsellor who worked sincerely with a client suffering from severe anxiety. The sessions were professional and well-intentioned. After a few meetings, the client suddenly stopped coming. Weeks later, a complaint surfaced, alleging that the counsellor had behaved "inappropriately." The allegation was entirely false. However, there was no written agreement, no documented informed consent, and no clear record of professional boundaries.

The counsellor eventually proved his innocence—but not before his reputation was damaged and his practice nearly collapsed before it had truly begun.

This story is unsettling, but it carries a lesson every counsellor must absorb early: good intentions alone do not offer protection. Compassion and skill are essential—but they are not enough. Clarity, boundaries, and legal safeguards are equally important. Just as a surgeon sterilises instruments before surgery, a counsellor must protect the therapeutic relationship with structures that prevent harm—both to the client and to the professional.

Why Legal Awareness Matters

Counselling works with emotions, memories, vulnerabilities, and at times, altered states of awareness. In such sensitive territory, misunderstandings are not rare—they are natural unless clear precautions are in place. A casually spoken sentence, a gesture meant as reassurance, or a client's distorted perception shaped by distress can later be interpreted very differently.

During the Covid period, I personally encountered this challenge. Clients called at all hours—late nights, early mornings, moments of panic and loneliness. Initially, my instinct was to be endlessly available. But I soon realised something important: without clearly defined boundaries, care can be misunderstood as special favour, and support can slowly turn into dependency.

It was during this phase that I consciously formalised my consent process and communication boundaries. Every client was clearly informed about session timings, emergency protocols, and the limits of availability. This did not reduce care—it strengthened it. Clients felt safer knowing what to expect, and I felt protected knowing the professional frame was clear.

Legal awareness is not about mistrust or cold professionalism. It is about safety. It protects the counsellor from false allegations and protects the client from any possibility—real or imagined—of exploitation or confusion.

Informed Consent: A Shield and a Bridge

One of the simplest and most powerful safety tools in counselling is the informed consent form. At first glance, it may look like mere paperwork. In reality, it serves two vital purposes.

It is a shield, because it documents that the client has understood the nature of counselling, the methods that may be used, the possible emotional discomforts, and the limits of confidentiality.

It is also a bridge, because it creates clarity. Expectations are stated openly at the beginning, preventing confusion, disappointment, or allegations later.

I never present consent forms as rigid legal contracts. I explain them in human terms. I tell clients,

"This document protects both of us. It helps you know what to expect from me, and it helps me stay firmly within ethical and professional boundaries."

In certain situations—especially when working with minors, adolescents, or individuals with psychiatric vulnerabilities—informed consent should also involve parents, guardians, or accompanying family members. This shared understanding reduces the risk of later misinterpretation and ensures transparency for everyone involved.

In counselling, clarity at the beginning is not bureaucracy. It is care expressed responsibly.

Indian Wisdom on Boundaries

The idea of boundaries in healing is not a modern legal invention. Long before consent forms and professional guidelines existed, Indian wisdom recognised that healing requires restraint as much as compassion.

In the *Charaka Samhita*, the physician is repeatedly advised to maintain dignity, self-discipline, and transparency in all interactions with patients. Healing was never meant to occur through emotional closeness alone, but within a framework that protected both the healer and the one seeking help. Respectful distance was seen not as coldness, but as ethical strength.

Similarly, the *Upanishads* describe the guru–shishya relationship as one grounded in reverence and discipline. While the bond was deeply personal, it was never casual. Clear rules governed conduct, speech, and behaviour, ensuring that intimacy in learning did not slip into familiarity or misuse.

Seen in this light, modern legal and ethical boundaries are not foreign to Indian thought. They are simply contemporary expressions of an age-old understanding: healing must always take place within structures that safeguard trust—protecting both the giver and the receiver of care.

Practical Scenarios and Precautions

When Misunderstanding Becomes Accusation

Over the course of my career, I have seen how even well-intentioned actions can be misunderstood when boundaries are not made explicit.

I recall a case where a counsellor guided a client through a relaxation exercise. To help the client refocus during a moment of restlessness, the counsellor lightly tapped the client's shoulder—a gesture meant purely as a grounding cue. No harm was intended. No discomfort was noticed at the time.

Later, however, the client described the experience to others as "unwanted touching."

The counsellor was shocked and deeply distressed. He insisted—truthfully—that the act was innocent and therapeutic. Yet in the absence of prior explanation and documented consent, intention alone was not enough to protect him. The allegation, though rooted in misunderstanding, gained credibility simply because boundaries had not been clearly established in advance.

This is why advance consent is non-negotiable.

If any form of physical technique may be used—even something seemingly minor such as a shoulder tap, a posture adjustment during guided breathing, or holding a hand during deep emotional release—the counsellor must obtain explicit verbal and written permission beforehand. Clients must be informed clearly and calmly:

"At certain points, I may use light physical contact to assist relaxation or grounding. This will only be done with your permission. Are you comfortable with this?"

Such clarity does not weaken the therapeutic relationship. It strengthens it. Clients feel safer when they know exactly what to expect, and counsellors are protected from misinterpretation.

In matters of boundaries, it is always better to explain too much than too little. Silence creates assumptions. Clarity creates safety.

Exploring the Subconscious: False Memory Concerns

In advanced counselling methods such as therapeutic meditation, guided imagery, or trance-based relaxation, clients may sometimes experience vivid inner imagery or strong emotional release. At times, memory-like fragments may surface—sensations, scenes, or impressions that *feel* real and emotionally charged.

It is important to understand that such experiences do not always represent factual memories. They may arise from imagination, symbolic association, subconscious material, or the mind's natural tendency to complete patterns when deeply relaxed. To the client, however, these experiences can feel as real as lived events.

Across the world, there have been cases where therapists were later accused of "implanting false memories," particularly in work involving trauma, childhood experiences, or subconscious exploration. Often, these accusations did not arise from malicious intent, but from confusion—when a client mistook an internally generated experience for an actual past event.

To prevent this risk, I make it a practice to explain this possibility clearly at the very beginning of therapy. I tell clients, both verbally and in writing:

"In rare cases, therapeutic processes may bring up experiences that feel like memories. These are not necessarily factual events. If such experiences occur, they are normal, reversible, and can be processed safely. Please inform me immediately so we can clarify and ground the experience together."

This clarification, included in the informed consent, protects the client from confusion and protects the counsellor from allegations of suggestion or manipulation.

A Simple Illustration: How False Memory Can Form

Consider a client who has poor appetite and is guided into a deep relaxed or trance-like state. During the session, the therapist gives a suggestion:

"You are feeling hungry now. You feel like eating."

The client readily agrees—because the subconscious mind responds strongly to suggestion in such states. If the therapist continues,

"Imagine you are eating a banana. It tastes good. You feel satisfied,"

the client may vividly experience the act of eating.

If asked later, "What kind of banana did you eat?" the client may describe it in detail—its taste, texture, even its sweetness. After the session, the client may still report the lingering taste of the banana.

At this point, a subtle confusion can arise:

Did I only imagine eating the banana, or did the therapist actually give it to me?

If this is not clarified, the mind may begin to construct a false belief—not out of deceit, but because the subconscious experience felt real.

This is how false memory can form: not through intentional manipulation, but through unexplained subjective experience.

The Counsellor's Responsibility

The counsellor's responsibility is not to avoid powerful techniques, but to frame them safely. Clients must be educated in advance that:

- subconscious experiences can feel real without being factual
- imagery is symbolic, not literal
- any confusion should be reported immediately
- clarification and grounding are always part of ethical practice

When clients are informed beforehand, they are far less likely to misinterpret their inner experiences—and far more likely to trust the process.

In subconscious work, clarity is not optional.

It is the line that separates healing from harm, and skill from risk.

Working with Psychiatric Illness: A Sensitive Zone

There are moments in counselling when emotional distress crosses into the territory of psychiatric illness. In such situations, the therapeutic space becomes especially delicate. The client may struggle with insight, misinterpret boundaries, or react unpredictably to structure and limits. What is meant as protection can sometimes be perceived as control; what is meant as support may be misunderstood as threat.

I recall a case in which a counsellor worked with a client who had a significant psychiatric condition. For safety and transparency, the counsellor insisted that a parent remain involved and present during sessions. The intention was ethical and protective. Yet the client later alleged "harassment," interpreting the boundary itself as mistreatment.

The counsellor was eventually vindicated—but only after weeks of emotional strain, anxiety, and damage to professional confidence. The experience left a deep impression on me.

Such situations do not arise from wrongdoing alone. They often arise from misinterpretation shaped by illness, especially when roles and expectations are not made unmistakably clear from the beginning.

For this reason, extra precautions are not optional when working in this sensitive zone.

I strongly advise the following practices when counselling individuals with significant psychiatric illness:

- Always inform and actively involve family members or caregivers, particularly when insight or judgement may be impaired.
- Ensure informed consent is signed by both the client and a responsible family member or guardian.
- Clarify explicitly that counselling is supportive and complementary, not a replacement for psychiatric diagnosis, medication, or medical treatment.

When these safeguards are in place, misunderstandings are far less likely. And if accusations do arise, there is already a shared, documented understanding of roles and boundaries.

In such cases, structure is not restriction.

It is protection—for everyone involved.

The Importance of Documentation

One of the simplest yet most powerful forms of protection for a counsellor is basic documentation.

Every session need not be recorded in exhaustive detail. But brief, consistent notes are essential: the date, duration, general themes discussed, and methods used. These notes are not meant to intrude on privacy—they exist to demonstrate professional transparency and continuity of care.

I was reminded of this during the Kerala floods, when I provided therapeutic meditation over the phone to families stranded in dangerous conditions. Amid chaos and urgency, I still noted the time of the call, the caller's name, and a brief summary of the intervention.

Not because I distrusted my clients—but because I understood that good records are a counsellor's safety net. They protect memory when recollection fades, and they protect integrity when questions arise later.

Documentation is not about suspicion.

It is about responsibility.

Indian Wisdom on Clarity and Trust

Indian wisdom has long understood that healing and guidance cannot flourish in ambiguity. Across traditions, clarity of role and intention was considered a moral responsibility—not an option.

In the *Vidura Niti* of the Mahabharata, Vidura repeatedly warns that confusion in conduct breeds mistrust, even when intentions are good. A guide who is unclear in word or action, he says, invites doubt—not because of wrongdoing, but because uncertainty itself unsettles the mind.

The *Arthashastra* goes a step further, insisting on clearly defined roles and limits for anyone in a position of authority or influence. Power without structure was seen as dangerous, not only to those being guided, but to the guide as well. Boundaries were described as safeguards that preserve trust and prevent misuse.

The *Bhagavad Gita* offers the same principle in psychological language. Krishna tells Arjuna that clarity of one's role dissolves confusion (*sammohah*). When role and responsibility are understood, fear reduces and trust stabilises. Where clarity is absent, anxiety multiplies.

Translated into modern counselling practice, this ancient wisdom carries a simple message: never allow confusion about what the client can expect from you. Transparency builds trust. And trust, when protected by clarity, prevents harm.

As I often tell my trainees:

"Healing is light. But light shines best when it is held within a clear lamp.

Boundaries are that lamp."

Without boundaries, even good intentions can cast shadows.

With them, healing remains steady, ethical, and safe.

Closing Reflections and Toolkit

The Counsellor's Double Duty

Counsellors often believe that their sole responsibility is the client's healing. In reality, there are two equally important duties: care for the client's well-being and care for the counsellor's own professional safety. Neglect either one, and the work begins to suffer.

Without safeguards, a counsellor may become vulnerable to false allegations, emotional exhaustion, or burnout caused by blurred boundaries. Without compassion, the client may feel unseen, misunderstood, or even harmed. The heart of ethical practice lies in balance.

Over more than five decades of practice, I learned this balance gradually—and sometimes painfully. Early generosity, offered without structure, once led to midnight calls that left me drained. At another time, the absence of written consent left me anxious about possible misinterpretation. These experiences taught me a crucial truth: legal awareness is not an obstacle to compassion—it is its ally.

Boundaries do not weaken trust; they deepen it. Clients feel safer when expectations are clear. Counsellors feel freer when their work rests on well-defined agreements. When both sides know the frame, healing can unfold without fear.

Closing Reflection: Healing with Clarity

Indian philosophy often compares the healer to a lamp. A lamp gives light—but only when its flame is protected by a steady glass enclosure. Without that protection, even the brightest flame can be extinguished by the slightest storm.

Clarity is the counsellor's glass frame. Informed consent, documentation, supervision, and appropriate family involvement are not bureaucratic chores. They are the quiet structures that allow compassion to burn longer, steadier, and brighter.

When healing and protection are honoured together, counselling becomes what it was always meant to be: a safe sanctuary where the human mind can open without fear. What begins as ethics in the heart must be completed with law in practice. Together, they allow the counsellor to work with warmth while standing on firm, unshakable ground.

Ethics and legal safeguards form the foundation of counselling—the inner compass and the outer shield. Yet counselling, like all living disciplines, must continue to evolve. As society changes, as technology reshapes human interaction, and as new challenges arise in families, schools, workplaces, and crises, counsellors too must adapt—without losing their ethical centre.

This brings us naturally to the final question:

How can counsellors prepare for the future while remaining rooted in timeless principles?

That question leads us to the concluding chapter—The Future of Counselling—where we explore the emerging trends, challenges, and opportunities that will shape the profession in the years to come.

Key Takeaways

- Legal awareness is as vital as therapeutic skill.
- Healing without protection places both client and counsellor at risk.
- Informed consent is foundational.
- It must clearly explain methods, boundaries, and possible risks—especially when working with touch, deep relaxation, or subconscious processes.
- False memories can occur without intention.
- Vivid images or sensations during therapy may feel real but are not necessarily factual. Clear explanation prevents confusion and allegations.
- Family involvement protects everyone.

- In cases involving minors or significant psychiatric illness, shared consent and transparency are essential.
- Documentation is professional self-care.
- Brief, factual session notes create continuity, clarity, and protection if questions arise later.
- Boundaries build trust, not distance.
- Clear limits around time, availability, and roles make the therapeutic space safer and more respectful.
- Indian wisdom supports ethical restraint.
- Ancient traditions emphasised clarity, discipline, and trust—principles that remain deeply relevant in modern counselling practice.

Practical Exercises

1. Consent Form Drafting

Take time to draft your own informed consent form, tailored to your style of practice. Clearly outline the purpose of counselling, the techniques you commonly use, possible emotional risks (such as intense emotional release or false-memory-like experiences), limits of confidentiality, and consent for physical contact if relevant. Where required, include space for family or guardian signatures.

As you write, ask yourself: *Would a client reading this feel informed, reassured, and respected?*

2. Boundary Role-Play

With a colleague or trainee partner, practise responding to situations where boundaries are tested—late-night calls, unscheduled visits, or repeated messages outside agreed hours. Focus not just on saying "no," but on how you say it. Notice how firmness can coexist with warmth, and how clarity can actually strengthen trust rather than weaken it.

3. Documentation Drill

After your next counselling session, write a brief professional note: date, duration, main concerns discussed, and techniques used. Avoid unnecessary detail but ensure enough clarity to reflect ethical and transparent practice. Review your notes and ask: *If read later, would this accurately and calmly represent my work?*

4. False Memory Explanation Practice

Practise explaining this gently to a mock client:

"Sometimes, therapy may bring up images, sensations, or feelings that resemble memories. These experiences can feel real but are not always literal events. If this happens, we will talk about it openly and process it safely together."

This rehearsal prepares you to respond with confidence and calm if such situations arise in real sessions.

5. Family Consent Simulation

Imagine working with a client who has a significant psychiatric condition. Draft how you would explain—respectfully and clearly—the need for family or guardian involvement in the consent process. Practise saying it aloud. Notice whether your explanation sounds protective rather than suspicious, collaborative rather than controlling.

Closing encouragement

These exercises are not about legal fear. They are about professional maturity. Each one strengthens your ability to care deeply while remaining grounded, protected, and clear.

When boundaries are practised consciously, they stop feeling restrictive—and start feeling supportive.

CHAPTER 12

SPECIAL INSIGHTS: MY EVOLVED TECHNIQUES

Over the years, I have often been asked, *"What is your method? What technique do you use?"*

It is an understandable question—especially in a world that values systems, steps, and formulas.

Yet the longer I have practised, the clearer one truth has become: counselling is never just a method. It is presence. It is listening beyond words. It is timing—knowing when to speak, when to remain silent, and when to offer a single sentence that can quietly change a life.

Still, across more than five decades of work, certain approaches have gradually taken shape. They were not planned or designed in advance. They emerged in moments of deep distress—during illness, grief, fear, or emotional collapse—when ordinary reassurance failed, but the subconscious mind responded instantly to an image, a reframe, or a carefully guided inner experience.

These are what I call my *evolved techniques*. They are not found neatly arranged in textbooks. They were shaped in real encounters, refined through human response, and validated by the sudden softening of pain or the return of hope.

This chapter brings together some of those approaches—once regarded as personal "secrets," rarely spoken about openly, but now shared here with one intention: to serve healing wherever it is needed.

Part 1 – The Power of Words and Metaphor

The subconscious mind does not always respond to logic or explanation. Often, it listens more closely to images, stories, and metaphors drawn from everyday life. A single sentence, if it touches the right inner chord, can do what hours of advice cannot.

I have seen this repeatedly—how the right metaphor, offered at the right moment, can bypass resistance and restore dignity, meaning, and calm.

The Old Man in the Old Age Home

An elderly man living in an old-age home came to me in deep distress. For days, he had been crying uncontrollably. His relatives—whom he had sacrificed everything for—had finally visited him after a year of silence. Instead of comfort, the visit reopened old wounds.

Through tears, he kept repeating,

"I gave them everything—my time, my money, my strength. And now I am left alone."

No argument could soothe him. No reassurance could touch the depth of his hurt. What he was mourning was not just abandonment—it was the loss of dignity.

I waited for the moment when his sobbing slowed, and then I said quietly:

"Think of a beggar. When we give to a beggar, his palm is always below ours. God has designed it this way—so that when you help someone, you are in the higher position, almost like God Himself. That is why you may never receive back from the same hands you once gave to. God will not allow you to become the beggar to those you helped. But blessings will come to you—from other directions, in other forms."

The change was immediate.

He stopped crying. He looked at me steadily, as if something within him had shifted place. Then he held my hands, kissed them gently, and said,

"I will never cry again over this."

What healed him was not advice or consolation.

It was a metaphor—one that transformed his pain into dignity, and his loss into meaning. His sorrow did not disappear, but it no longer humiliated him.

That is the quiet power of the right words, spoken at the right time.

Part 2 – Therapeutic Meditation and Subconscious Reframing in Crises

Over the years, therapeutic meditation emerged as one of my most effective tools during moments of crisis. In times of illness, disaster, or profound grief—when logic collapses and the body is overwhelmed by emotion—words alone are often insufficient. But through voice, guided imagery, and carefully chosen reframes, it becomes possible to calm the nervous system and gently awaken the mind's own capacity to heal.

In such moments, the counsellor does not argue with pain. Instead, the counsellor offers the subconscious a new way to hold it.

The Old Lady and the Two Birds

An eighty-year-old widow was brought to me after the death of her husband. Her grief was relentless. She cried day after day, her body shaking with sobs. Throat cancer had taken away her voice, so she communicated by writing on a small pad she held tightly in her hands.

On one such page, she wrote:

"We lived like two birds together. But God shot one. Why not me?"

Her grief was not only about loss—it was about injustice.

I sat with her quietly until her breathing slowed, and then I asked a single question:

"If you were born again, whom would you choose to marry—your husband again, or another man?"

Without hesitation, she scribbled back:

"Only him."

I then said gently:

"If you had died first, your husband would have been reborn younger than you. Society would never have allowed you to marry him again. God understood your love. So He took him first—so that in the next life, you could reunite freely."

The change was immediate.

Her sobbing stopped as suddenly as if someone had pulled an emergency brake. The tension in her body softened. The story of her loss had shifted—from cruelty to meaning.

Her grief did not vanish. But it transformed into peace.

The Couple Who Wouldn't Let Their Son Go

Another encounter involved a middle-aged couple who had lost their only son of 26 years old in a sudden accident. Months had passed, yet time seemed frozen inside their home. They sat together every day, crying, replaying memories, refusing to move forward.

"We feel his soul here," they told me. "We don't want him to leave us."

Their love had turned into invisible chains.

I spoke to them using the language of their own faith and understanding.

"In our tradition," I said, "every soul must move toward *moksha*. If you hold him tightly with grief, his journey remains incomplete. Love does not bind—it releases."

I paused, then added softly:

"If you truly love him, let your love become a blessing, not a burden. Release him with joy, so his soul may move freely."

Something shifted.

Their tears slowed. Their grief softened into devotion. In the days that followed, they chose to perform rituals, charity, and acts of service in their son's name. Their mourning was no longer an act of holding back—it became an act of love that allowed both them and their son to move forward.

Therapeutic meditation and subconscious reframing do not deny pain. They change the meaning that pain carries. When meaning changes, suffering loosens its grip—and healing finds a way in.

Healing at the Edge of Life

She was a woman in the final stage of cancer, exhausted by pain that even morphine could no longer touch. Her body lay still, but her eyes were sharp with bitterness when she looked at me.

"What is the use of counselling," she asked quietly, "when I am only waiting for death's bell?"

I did not argue with her fear. I spoke gently, honestly.

"If twenty of us stood in this room," I said, "could any of us predict who would die first? None of us can. Death is not in our control. What *is* in our control is how peacefully we live the time we have. I cannot change the number of your days—but I may be able to give you peace in this moment."

She listened. After a pause, she nodded.

Through hypnosis, I guided her into a state of deep calm—slowing her breath, easing the tension her body had been holding for so long. Within twenty minutes, the pain that had dominated her awareness softened and then receded.

She opened her eyes and said, almost with surprise,

"Please stay. I feel peaceful… after such a long time."

At the edge of life, counselling did not promise cure.

It offered dignity, relief, and a moment of peace—and that, too, is healing.

When the Mind Heals the Body

Another man, sixty years old, had been confined to his bed for eleven years. After a brain tumour scare, he had lost the use of both legs. Though his limbs appeared healthy, fear had settled deep into his nervous system. Movement had become unthinkable.

When I met him, I spoke plainly:

"The mind that holds fear can also hold healing. If you follow me carefully, we will try to awaken that strength."

He looked at me steadily and said,

"I will do whatever you say."

During a forty-five–minute session focused on subconscious activation—calming fear, restoring confidence, and reconnecting mind and body—I asked him to imagine standing, then rising.

When the session ended, I asked him gently to try.

To the astonishment of everyone present, he stood—and then walked slowly, completing three rounds of the room. Tears followed, not from pain, but from disbelief.

Today, he continues to walk with the support of a walker. His body had not forgotten how to move. It was his mind that had needed permission to trust again.

When Pain Speaks the Language of the Mind

A young schoolgirl in the ninth standard was brought to me after forty-five days of relentless stomach pain. Medical tests revealed nothing. The pain was real, yet unexplained. Her cries were so intense that even a psychologist had turned her away, unable to bear her distress.

When she arrived, I did not interrupt or analyse. I let her speak—freely, endlessly—until the storm inside her began to quiet.

Then I guided her gently into a trance state, offering therapeutic suggestions aimed not at the pain itself, but at the emotions beneath it. Gradually, her breathing slowed. Her body relaxed. The pain dissolved.

She opened her eyes and smiled - as if waking from a long, frightening dream.

Her body had not been lying.

It had been speaking the only language it knew.

Once her mind was finally heard, her body no longer needed to cry out.

At the edges of life—where medicine hesitates and logic falls silent, the mind often speaks in symbols, pain, and fear. When listened to with care, it can also guide the way back to peace.

CONCLUSION

Healing as Wholeness

As this book comes to a close, it is worth pausing to reflect on the deeper arc that has unfolded across these chapters. Counselling, as explored here, is not merely a professional intervention or a collection of techniques. It is a human journey—one that moves through fear, confusion, resistance, insight, and ultimately, integration.

Across decades of practice, one truth has become increasingly clear to me: healing is rarely about fixing what is "broken." More often, it is about restoring balance where fear has taken over, clarity where confusion has settled, and confidence where trauma has quietly eroded strength. Whether the struggle presents itself as anxiety, grief, addiction, relationship conflict, illness, or inner emptiness, the underlying need remains the same—to feel safe again within oneself.

Modern life, with all its advancements, has intensified psychological strain. People carry invisible burdens: unspoken grief, unresolved trauma, suppressed anger, chronic stress, and existential uncertainty. Counselling offers a structured yet compassionate space where these burdens can be acknowledged without judgment. It allows the mind to speak, the body to settle, and the subconscious to release what it has been holding in silence.

Throughout this book, we have seen that healing does not follow a straight line. Resistance appears. Fear resurfaces. Old patterns return. Yet none of these are failures. They are part of the natural rhythm of transformation. Counselling works not by force, but by presence—by meeting the client exactly where they are and walking with them until they are ready to walk alone.

One experience, among many, reflects this understanding with particular clarity.

A person undergoing treatment for abdominal cancer received regular medical care alongside ongoing counselling and therapeutic meditation, conducted at intervals of five to seven days. Surgically, the lower part of the large intestine had been removed, followed by a structured course of chemotherapy. Medically, the treatment plan was clear and necessary. Psychologically, however, the individual was carrying a deep and often unspoken trauma—the shock of diagnosis, the fear of mortality, the loss of bodily control, and the prolonged state of inner threat that accompanies serious illness.

Serious disease does not affect the body alone. It disrupts the entire psycho-biological system. Persistent fear and unresolved trauma activate chronic stress responses, altering biochemical balance, straining the nervous system, and weakening immune coordination. Through counselling, these emotional layers were gently addressed. Through therapeutic meditation, the body was repeatedly guided back into states of calm, safety, and internal coherence.

Over time, as fear softened and emotional regulation improved, the individual's physiological responses also began to shift. Sleep became deeper and more restorative. Appetite and energy stabilised. Cooperation with treatment improved. Notably, many of the commonly anticipated side effects of chemotherapy either did not appear at all or, when they did emerge, subsided more quickly and with less intensity than expected. This change was not accidental; it reflected a body no longer locked in continuous stress response, but one able to support healing rather than resist it.

Later, this was expressed simply and profoundly by the individual:

"Medicine treated the disease, but counselling and meditation helped my body accept the treatment."

This distinction is important. Counselling did not replace medicine. Therapeutic meditation did not claim to cure cancer. Their role was to remove psychological and biochemical resistance—allowing the immune system to function with greater precision and enabling medical treatment to work under more favourable internal conditions.

Equally significant was the restoration of confidence. Before the illness, this individual had been capable, talented, and self-assured. Like many who face major disease, the trauma of diagnosis and treatment had eroded these qualities. Even after physical recovery, confidence often remains fragile, leaving individuals medically "well" but psychologically diminished.

In this case, counselling and therapeutic meditation addressed that deeper loss. By working through fear, vulnerability, and unconscious threat, confidence did not merely return to its earlier level—it reorganised itself more deeply. The individual emerged with greater emotional stability, clearer self-trust, and a renewed sense of purpose. Illness no longer defined identity; it had been integrated rather than endured.

From a psycho-biological perspective, this restoration matters. Confidence is not only an attitude—it reflects a regulated nervous system, balanced stress chemistry, and a body no longer trapped in survival mode. As fear recedes, physiological resources shift from defence toward repair, recovery, and growth.

This experience reinforces a central conviction that has guided my work for decades: true healing is not only the absence of disease, but the restoration of confidence, clarity, and inner strength—sometimes at a level deeper than before the crisis.

Responsibility and Restraint

Equally important is an understanding of what counselling is *not*. It is not omnipotence. It is not moral authority. It is not endless availability. The chapters on ethics and self-care underline a truth that experienced practitioners eventually learn: to help well, one must also know when to step back.

Boundaries protect not only the counsellor, but the client. Referral, supervision, and rest are not signs of inadequacy; they are expressions of professionalism. A counsellor who respects their own limits models psychological health far more powerfully than one who pretends to have none.

In this sense, counselling is an ethical discipline as much as a therapeutic one. It requires clarity of role, transparency of intention, and a constant awareness of power—how it can heal, and how easily it can harm if left unchecked.

Wisdom That Transcends Time

The integration of Indian philosophical insights alongside modern psychological understanding is not an intellectual exercise; it reflects lived reality. Long before counselling became a profession, human beings grappled with fear, duty, loss, and inner conflict. The language has changed, but the experience has not.

These traditions remind us that hesitation is not failure, that inner conflict is not pathology, and that clarity often arrives gradually. Counselling, at its best, honours this pace. It does not rush the person toward resolution; it accompanies them until resolution becomes possible.

For Those Who Read This Book

If you are a practitioner, may this book affirm what experience has already taught you: that presence matters as much as knowledge, and humility as much as competence.

If you are a learner, may it encourage you to study psychology not only with your intellect, but with your awareness.

If you are a leader, parent, or caregiver, may you recognise that listening—without immediately correcting—can transform relationships.

And if you are someone carrying unseen weight, may you take this with you: struggle does not disqualify you from wholeness. Understanding, when it arrives in the right moment, can restore balance in ways that force never can.

A Journey That Continues

Counselling does not conclude with closure; it continues in how people live afterward—in the choices they make, the pauses they allow, and the compassion they extend to themselves and others. The counsellor's task is never to walk the path for another, but to ensure they are no longer lost when they walk it alone.

If these pages have offered anything of value, let it be a quiet confidence in the human capacity to heal, adapt, and grow—when met with patience, respect, and genuine presence.

In the end, counselling is not about having the right answers.

It is about being willing to stay with the question—together—until clarity finds its own voice.

BIBLIOGRAPHY

Ader, R. (Ed.). (2007). *Psychoneuroimmunology.* San Diego: Academic Press.

Bandura, A. (1977). *Social Learning Theory.* Englewood Cliffs, NJ: Prentice Hall.

Beck, A. T. (1976). *Cognitive Therapy and the Emotional Disorders.* New York: International Universities Press.

Benedetti, F. (2014). *Placebo Effects.* Oxford: Oxford University Press.

Benson, H., & Proctor, W. (2010). *Relaxation Revolution.* New York: Scribner.

Corey, G. (2017). *Theory and Practice of Counseling and Psychotherapy* (10th ed.). Boston: Cengage Learning.

Ellis, A. (1994). *Reason and Emotion in Psychotherapy.* Secaucus, NJ: Birch Lane.

Erickson, M. H., Rossi, E. L., & Rossi, S. I. (1976). *Hypnotic Realities.* New York: Irvington.

Everly, G. S., & Mitchell, J. T. (2008). *The Critical Incident Stress Management Approach.* Ellicott City, MD.

Frankl, V. E. (1946). *Man's Search for Meaning.* Boston: Beacon Press.

Goleman, D. (1995). *Emotional Intelligence.* New York: Bantam Books.

Grossman, P., & Taylor, E. W. (2007). Toward understanding respiratory sinus arrhythmia. *Biological Psychology, 74,* 263–285.

Hammond, D. C. (Ed.). (1990). *Handbook of Hypnotic Suggestions and Metaphors.* New York: Norton.

Hanson, R. (2013). *Hardwiring Happiness.* New York: Harmony Books.

Kabat-Zinn, J. (2013). *Full Catastrophe Living.* New York: Bantam.

Kirsch, I. (1999). *How Expectancies Shape Experience.* Washington, DC: American Psychological Association.

Lakoff, G., & Johnson, M. (2003). *Metaphors We Live By.* Chicago: University of Chicago Press.

Lynn, S. J., Kirsch, I., Barabasz, A., Cardeña, E., & Patterson, D. (2000). Hypnosis as an empirically supported intervention. *International Journal of Clinical and Experimental Hypnosis, 48*(2), 239–259.

McAdams, D. P. (2001). The psychology of life stories. *Review of General Psychology, 5*(2), 100–122.

Porges, S. W. (2011). *The Polyvagal Theory.* New York: Norton.

Roberts, N. P., et al. (2009). Early psychological interventions for trauma. *Journal of Consulting and Clinical Psychology, 77*(3), 507–520.

Rossman, M. L. (2000). *Guided Imagery for Self-Healing.* Novato, CA: New World Library.

Rogers, C. R. (1961). *On Becoming a Person.* Boston: Houghton Mifflin.

Sarno, J. E. (1998). *The Mindbody Prescription.* New York: Warner Books.

Seligman, M. E. P. (2011). *Flourish.* New York: Free Press.

Thayer, J. F., & Lane, R. D. (2000). A model of neurovisceral integration. *Biological Psychology, 74*, 263–285.

van der Kolk, B. (2014). *The Body Keeps the Score.* New York: Viking.

White, M., & Epston, D. (1990). *Narrative Means to Therapeutic Ends.* New York: Norton.

Yalom, I. D. (1980). *Existential Psychotherapy.* New York: Basic Books.

www.ingramcontent.com/pod-product-compliance
Lightning Source LLC
LaVergne TN
LVHW100309210926
848480LV00003B/1068
* 9 7 9 8 9 0 3 4 2 2 7 6 0 *